GET
RICH
NOW

Other books by Brian Tracy

Entrepreneurship

Make More Money

The Phoenix Transformation

The 10 Qualities of Influential People

Get It Done Now!

GET RICH NOW

Earn More Money, Faster and Easier Than Ever Before

BRIAN TRACY

MEDIA

Published 2022 by Gildan Media LLC
aka G&D Media
www.GandDmedia.com

Front cover design by David Rheinhardt of Pyrographx

Interior design by Meghan Day Healey of Story Horse, LLC

Library of Congress Cataloging-in-Publication Data is available upon request

ISBN: 978-1-7225-0599-8

10   9   8   7   6   5   4   3   2   1

CONTENTS

FOREWORD

Money remains one of the most thought-provoking, emotional, and polarizing subjects in the world. Scores of books, articles, blog posts, and speeches have been written on what money is, how to earn it, how to spend it, who has it and who does not, and a myriad of other topics. And yet, despite this constant focus, there is one word that describes the average person's views about money: *confusion.*

Despite the great research that has been published on the topic, there is much misinformation—what we might call financial white noise—about money. As a result, most people either rely on chance for their fortune or ignore the subject altogether. This is a tragedy. People leave a great deal of their potential untapped when they turn their lives over to chance, or worse, give up on their dreams. It's totally unnecessary, because the secrets of money, how to create it, how to invest it, and how to spend it wisely, *are known.*

In this book, Brian will be examining both the laws of money, which have been proven and can be relied upon, and the myths about money. Myths include ideas that exist without any basis. They claim to be true but have been tested and disproven, or, at best, have never been decidedly proven.

This book has one central goal: to end the confusion around the topic once and for all, and to present the essential truths about money in one comprehensive place. If you study these ideas and apply them to your life and your business, you will become financially successful as surely as the sun will rise tomorrow.

Goal of this book: To end the confusion around money once and for all, and to present the essential truths about money in one comprehensive place.

ONE

What Is Money?

The first law of money is the *law of exchange*: money is the medium through which people exchange their labor in the production of goods and services for the goods and services of others. Money is a medium of exchange for labor.

Before there was money, there was barter. People directly exchanged goods and services for other goods and services without the medium of money. In prehistoric times, someone would make a flint spearhead or a pot and exchange it for a carpet or a skin.

As civilization grew, barter became too clumsy. People found that they could exchange their goods and services for a medium like gold, silver, coins, seashells, wampum—something that was scarce and valuable. People would have an item of value, which they could exchange for a chicken or a goat or something else they wanted. It makes the whole process more efficient.

That was the beginning of money, and it still defines what money is today, even though many people are very confused about it. Money makes the process of exchange more efficient. Today we go to work and we exchange our work for money, which we then use to purchase the products of the work of other people. Money is the medium through which we exchange our work for the work of others.

The first corollary of the law of exchange is that money is a measure of the value that people place on goods and services. It's only what a person will pay that determines the value of something. Things do not have value in and of themselves. Goods and services have no value apart from what someone is willing to pay for them. You can't say that your product or service is worth a given amount unless somebody else validates it by actually offering you that amount of money. All value is therefore subjective. This is the basis of the Austrian school, which is the most insightful school of economics in history. Value is based on the thoughts, feelings, attitudes, and opinions of the prospective purchaser at the moment of buying.

The second corollary of the law of exchange says that your labor is viewed as a factor of production, that is, as a cost, by others. This demolishes almost all of the economic arguments about whether people should be paid $15 an hour or something else. One name for human beings is *Homo economicus*. This means that we always act economically: we always try to get the very most for the very least. This is genetic; it's built into our

---

"Money is the medium through which we exchange our work for the work of others."

DNA. It has never been otherwise in all of human history. We never will pay more if we can possibly pay less.

Each of us tends to look upon the sweat of our brow as something special, because it's so intensely personal; it comes from us. It expresses who we are as persons. It's very emotional, because it's our life. But as far as others are concerned, our labor is just a cost. As intelligent consumers, employers, or customers, we want the very most for the very least, no matter whose labor is involved. This is why people manufacture in China, Taiwan, Vietnam, or Indonesia. The customer in America does not care where the product comes from. The customer simply cares about getting the lowest price.

People talk about offshoring: sending jobs overseas. It's not the companies, it's the customers that are demanding that they send these jobs there, because the products and services can be produced at a lower cost. Until very recently, almost all of Apple's products were made in China. Why? It's because the cost to manufacture them in a more developed country is three or four times the amount it costs in China, so the customers in developed countries will not pay that amount. They demand—indirectly—that companies offshore these jobs so that they can have the most for the least.

For this reason, you can't place an objective value on your own labor, protesting and demanding increases. It's only what other people are willing to pay for your labor in a competitive market that determines what you earn and what you are worth in financial terms.

The third corollary of this law says the amount of money you earn is a measure of the value that others place on your contribution. In other words, the customers in the marketplace determine what we're worth. The customers of the companies that we work for determine what they will pay for the products and services that we contribute to the production. This in turn determines how much we will be paid. There's no *objective* amount that we can be paid. How much you are paid will be in direct proportion to the quantity and quality of your contribution in comparison with the contributions of others, combined with the value that other people place on your contributions.

One thing I used to say is that you are competing every single day with every other person in your company. People would get really huffy about that; they'd say, "We don't compete; we all work together as team members." Yet the person who determines your paycheck determines how much you will be paid in comparison with how much other people are paid. That's why most companies have a rule that you're not allowed to discuss your pay with other people, because your pay is determined by what the company thinks you are worth relative to everyone else working around you.

The fourth corollary of the law of exchange is that money is an effect, not a cause. Your work or contribution to the value of a product or service is the cause, and the wage, salary, or earnings that you receive are the effect. If you wish to increase the effect, you have to increase the cause. As inspirational speaker Earl Nightingale said years ago, the law of cause and effect is the foundational law of all of human life—all science, all technology, all mathematics, all money.

The fifth corollary of the law of exchange is that to increase the amount of money you are getting out, you must increase the value of the work that you are putting in. People think that they can get more out without putting more in. If you ask, "Where's

> **"How much you are paid will be in direct proportion to the quantity and quality of your contribution in comparison with the contributions of others, combined with the value that other people place on your contributions."**

the money going to come from?" their answer is, "Somewhere." If you press them, they say, "Well, the money should come from other people who are creating more value, who therefore are earning more. Then they should give it to me—even though, according to the market, I'm creating less value—so that I don't feel bad." This attitude—that I'm entitled to more money—is nonsense. That's why it leads to riots and strikes and similar disruptions.

To earn more money, you must add more value. The secret to wealth creation is to add value. Sometimes I ask people how many of them work on straight commission. I'll ask 1,000 people, and about 10 or 15 percent of people will raise their hands. The truth is, *everybody* works on straight commission. What does that mean? It means everybody gets a percentage of the value that they create. If you're not happy with the percentage that you're getting, create more value and become worth more. Your boss or your customers will willingly pay you more, because they value your contribution more.

Some people earn $10 an hour; some people earn $1,000 an hour. I have a friend who upgraded his skills from being a commercial lawyer to being a lawyer in intellectual copyright, a field nobody was in. It was a white space. Companies like Sony and Disney and the biggest companies in the world eagerly pay him $1,000 an hour to help them with intellectual property law, because the amounts involved are hundreds of millions of dollars, and he's an expert. He made himself so valuable that they get in line to pay him whatever he wants. He is often paid $2 million or $3 million to vet a single contract or merger between companies that have intellectual property, such as movie companies.

To earn more money, you must add more value, so you must increase your knowledge. As management expert Peter Drucker said, we're all knowledge workers, so by increasing your knowledge of how to do your business better, you increase your value. People will then be willing and eager to thrust money into your hand. Or you increase your skill level so that you can get more and better work done in the same period of time. Or you improve your work habits so that you're far more productive.

The highest-paid people in every society and every business are always result-oriented. They are highly productive. I have worked with people and taught them nothing other than time management skills, and they've tripled their income in less than a year, doing the same job for the same company. The company willingly gives them more money because they're producing vastly more value.

To make more money, you can work longer and harder hours. The most successful people always work much harder than others. In fact, statistics say that about fifty-nine to sixty hours a week puts you in the top 20 percent. If you work seventy hours a week, you'll be in the top 5 or 10 percent. The average person today works a forty-hour week, but according to the labor studies, during that week they only work thirty-two hours. Why? They take coffee breaks and lunches; they start later and stop earlier. They waste 50 percent of those thirty-two hours, mostly with idle chitchat, Facebook, social media,

Internet, and phoning friends. The average person is only doing sixteen hours of productive work each week, and in that time they do work of low value. But they don't understand why they don't get paid more money.

The secret to success is to work all the time you work. Start earlier, work harder, stay later, and work the whole time. Don't mess around. Don't chat with your friends. Don't go out for lunch or coffee, read the paper, or surf the Internet. When you come to work, work. Put your head down full blast and work.

You can also work more creatively, or you can do anything that enables you to get greater leverage and results from your efforts. Some people produce five times as much as other people in the same eight hours a day.

The 5 Corollary's of The Law of Exchange

1. Money is a measure of value that people place on goods and services.
2. Your labor is viewed as a factor of production, that is, as a cost, by others.
3. The amount of money you earn is a measure of the value that others place on your contribution.
4. Money is an effect, not a cause.
5. To increase the amount of money you are getting out, you must increase the value of work that you are putting in.

By the way, all wealthy people work six days a week. This is shown in study after study. It's not hard to work six days a week.

If you're doing work that you really enjoy and you're doing it really well and you're getting great results, you get pumped up. It makes you happy. In fact, successful people have to use self-discipline to *not* work because they like their work so much.

Your responsibility is to find work that you enjoy so much that it gives you so much energy that you have to force yourself to stop. For people who are doing the right work, time stands still. They forget to eat. They forget to take breaks. They forget to go for coffee. They're so engrossed in their work that they have to be torn away to eat.

The highest-paid people in our society are those who are continually improving in these areas so that they add greater value to the work they're doing. The amount you earn is a direct reflection of the value that you create to improve the life and work of other people. All success in life comes from serving other people in some way. If you want to make a lot of money, serve a lot of people, and serve them in a way that really makes a difference to them.

Today many people are complaining about the salaries of CEOs, which are so much larger than those of ordinary employees, and the golden parachutes CEOs get when they leave. Or they say, "Look at the stock market. There are those who use the market like a casino. They roll the dice and make money when the stock market goes down or up."

Most people are abysmally ignorant about money, so they believe in fantastical things. It reminds me of the cargo cults of the South Pacific. During the Second World War, the Allies came into New Guinea, built airfields, and set up military bases to counter the Japanese. Then the military would bring in food, clothing, and other necessities for the troops. All of their supplies came in by these planes. When the war was over, they withdrew, and New Guinea went back to the jungle.

The natives in these areas who were used as workers during the war had no idea where the wealth came from. They believed that wealth came from the cargo planes. They started cargo cults. They would build little dolls and little models of planes, and they would put them on little altars. They would light incense and pray to them, worship them, and sing. They would pray for the planes to come back with the wealth inside.

This is about as intelligent as people's complaints about stock market speculators. With regard to stock market speculation, you will find that the highest-paid people who work in the stock market work hard for that pay. For example, billionaire Warren Buffett spends 80 percent of his time every day studying the stock market, companies, and changing fortunes in competition. He's ninety-two years old. He goes to work, puts his head down, and studies these investments. He started off with $2,000, and he used what is called the *value investing model*. He studies the inherent value of the company's products, services, management, and positioning in the industry compared to national and international competition.

On the other hand, most of the people who jump in and out of the stock end up broke. It's like the professional poker players who go off to Las Vegas to make a lot of money. They find they would earn as much if they had a laboring job at the end of the day, because with the amount they win and the amount they lose, they make a few dollars an hour sitting at the poker tables for twelve or fourteen hours.

In the stock market, day traders and flash traders, who are in and out and in and out—70 percent of them eventually are wiped out. A client once introduced me to a man who had spent several hundred million dollars developing a fifty-person flash trading organization. I saw it: huge screens, brilliant mathematicians day-trading in and out of stocks, trying to get fractions of pennies here and there. He put in several hundred million dollars, and he lost it all. At the end of the day, all these people working full-time sixteen hours a day lost everything and just walked away. Fortunately, he was a multi-billionaire, so he could afford to lose several hundred million dollars on something speculative.

Most people who make money in stocks are long-term players. Warren Buffett buys a stock and holds it for fifty years. He's a value trader. Every so often he will sell part of a holding, but usually to raise cash to purchase something else that is getting a better return at this point.

As for golden parachutes, when an executive is lured away to take a job in a Fortune 500 company, they are offered very high pay, with stock options, and their lawyers negotiate these contracts. They also negotiate severance pay. If something doesn't work out and the company decides that it doesn't want them anymore for any reason, they pay severance. People say, "Executives get golden parachutes." Yes, those are the terms under which they took the job, and they took the job coming from somewhere else where they also had fantastic jobs. This was just a normal part of it.

Today presidents of the Fortune 500 earn an average of 303 times the average pay of the people who work in their corporations. But at the beginnings of their careers, all these people, like marathon runners, started off at the same starting line. At the beginning, these executives were the same as everybody

---

Most people who make money in stocks are long-term players, not stock speculators or day traders.

---

else. They started off in their jobs and were put into pools or cubicles. Some of them had good educations; some had average educations. Some of them had gotten straight A's; some hadn't. Some of them came from good homes, some from poor homes. Some were Mayflower descendants, and some were new immigrants that didn't speak the language when they started. Today these executives earn 303 times the pay of the average worker. That's about $10.3 million in annual salary, while the average person in their companies makes $52,000.

How could that be? From the beginning of their careers, the successful people asked this question: what one skill would help me make a more valuable contribution at this point in my career? They would go to their boss, and the boss would say, "If you were really good at marketing, or reading financial statements, or doing presentations, or building teams, or negotiating, you could be more valuable in your job."

These people would set that as a project, and put together a learning plan, like going to school. They would find out the best books to read, the best audio programs to listen to, the best courses to take, and the best things to do to develop these skills. After six months or a year, they would have developed them, because all business skills are learnable.

The magic number is ten hours a week. While their friends were out socializing and chasing boys or girls, these people would spend an average of two hours per day, five days per week, upgrading their skills. It became as natural to them as breathing in and breathing out. They came home at night, had dinner with their spouses and children, and studied two hours per night, five days a week.

Once when I was speaking in India, I said, "I'm not that familiar with your time zones, but how many hours are there in an average week here in India?" They all laughed at me. I said, "Yeah, it's 168 hours: seven times twenty-four. Could you carve off ten hours per week to become one of the wealthiest, highest-paid, most respected people in your industry?" They said, "Yes, of course you can." It's just simply a matter of willpower and self-discipline.

Furthermore, each new skill is subject to the law of compounding. Each new skill enables you to use your other skills at a higher level. You can increase your earning ability, your ability to make a contribution. You can be worth more because you can get better results. You become more valuable, so people pay you more and promote you faster.

The cumulative effect is like an avalanche. After ten or twenty or thirty years, you're in your forties and fifties, and you're earning 303 times the average of other people who have not raised a finger to learn a thing since they took their first job. How come these people are paid so much? Some say, "They're just lucky." But these people make decisions that affect hundreds of millions of dollars, sometimes billions of dollars. They can make a decision to go in and out of an industry, to sell off a division or an entire series of factories, and the impact of that on the bottom line may be $1 billion. What do they get? They get $10 million. They get a fraction of 1 percent of the total economic impact of their decisions. But they started off working alone with a small assignment

---

What one skill would help me make a more valuable contribution at this point in my career?

---

in a cubicle with a little laptop. Now they're running huge businesses, and their offices take up the top floors of the best office buildings.

Everybody had the ability to do that, and everybody still has the ability to do something similar.

People often ask me, "What was your great motivation when you started?" My answer is, to eat. When I took my first job, I wanted to make enough money to eat. My first job was washing dishes. I lived in a one-room apartment that had a stovetop on top, a refrigerator down below, a bathroom with a cheap shower, and a bed. I was a laborer and couldn't afford any more than that. I drove an old car. I wore old clothes. I worked eight to ten hours a day, and all I thought about was survival.

I had a couple of good experiences. When I was twelve years old, I found that I could get jobs in the neighborhood cutting grass and mowing lawns. My parents eventually encouraged me to get a gas-powered lawn mower. They took me down to Sears and got me an absolutely dreadful lawn mower, because they didn't know anything about it.

I would push this mower around the neighborhood and mow lawns. Pretty soon I was doing really well, and I decided to get a better mower. I began to hang around a lawn mower shop. I looked at the models they had and bought a used commercial lawn mower that was fabulous. It was the same kind of machine they used to cut golf greens. It was beautiful, and it threw the grass forward so it left no marks on the lawn.

Then I began to mow even more lawns. People began to recommend me because their lawns looked beautiful. Then I got a trimmer to do sidewalks and the flowerbeds. Then I got a little cart to pull it around on. By the time I was fifteen, I was earning more money than my father was, pulling my little cart around and mowing lawns, even for the mayor of the city.

From this experience, I learned there was a direct association between hard work and ingenuity on the one hand and your income on the other. The sooner you make the connection between your work and your income, the more likely you are to be successful.

Later I went back and worked in factories, mills, and construction. When I could no longer get a laboring job, I went back into selling. I used to sell my lawn mowing services door-to-door. I sold soap, newspaper subscriptions, Christmas books. At that time I was paid on straight commission. The joke, we used to say, is that you can only eat what you kill. If you don't make a sale, you don't eat, which is one of the great motivators.

I understood that my income was totally determined by my ability to get results that people would pay me for. What is your most valuable financial asset? Your earning ability: your ability to get results that people will pay you for. The most important word for success in life and business is *results*. The people who get results are the most respected and esteemed people in every area of life.

You might say that *results* sounds very cold. But even with your family, it's a matter of results: building a solid marriage and raising happy, healthy, self-confident children.

Your earning ability is an asset, and like all assets, it can be appreciating or depreciating in value. If it's appreciating, you are becoming worth more and more every day.

> **Your earning ability—your ability to get results that people will pay you for—is your most valuable financial asset.**

There was a story in *Fortune* about a woman who worked for the magazine for forty-six years. She retired in her seventies. She was one of the most esteemed people there. They had big parties to see her off. They asked her why she had been so valuable to the magazine for all those years. She said, "Because I resolved never to go to bed at night without being smarter than I was when I woke up that day. Every single day I learned something new that would help me do my job better."

This woman interviewed Fortune 500 CEOs and presidents and the leading financial lights of the world. She could phone Warren Buffett or Bill Gates, and they'd take her calls, because she was so highly esteemed. That's earning ability.

If you ask the average person, "What have you done today to increase your value, to increase your ability to get results and add more value to your world?" they will be shocked. Yet Einstein said that compounding is the greatest power in the universe. Compounding means each time you add to your skills, it combines with other knowledge you have, and sooner or later all these pieces of information come together. It's called the *law of integrative intelligence*. All these pieces of intelligence start to integrate and form a pattern that enable you to see an opportunity to create wealth that you hadn't seen before. Sometimes one additional piece of information transforms everything, bringing together all the knowledge that you've been gathering for a long time. Suddenly it all clicks, and you have a new product or service that is transformative.

Look at Steve Jobs and Apple: he came up with the idea of the iPod. All of the technology for the iPod had existed and had been sold by other companies. He created a new business model.

Today there are fifty-five different types of business models. If you have the wrong one, your company will drift and often go broke. Business models are changing so fast that 80 percent or more of companies, including Fortune 500 companies, have broken or obsolete business models.

A new business model brings together a number of different factors in a manner that transforms everything. Google is a perfect example. They linked hundreds and thousands of computers so that people could search for information free. While people were on the site, they could buy a product or service, and Google could use algorithms to track the things they were interested in and make ads for those things pop up. Google created one of the most valuable companies in the world with its new business model. They offered the finest services in the world absolutely free, saying "By the way, while you're here, here's something else that you may want."

Your earning ability is the most important thing of all, and again, it's either appreciating or depreciating. Basketball coach Pat Riley once said that either you're getting better or you're getting worse. Nobody stays the same. Every new skill that you develop moves you up the ladder of earning ability. Every new skill means that you are worth more money. Each time you learn a new skill, you step up the ladder; your earning ability increases. If you keep climbing the ladder, your earning ability keeps increasing.

The highest-paid people today are those who keep climbing skill by skill, day by day, week by week, month by month. They never stop learning new skills. They keep becoming more and more valuable. As a result, other people eagerly thrust money in their pockets and pay them millions of dollars to take senior jobs and pay them millions more in severance pay if they leave.

The question you always have to ask is, "What have I done today to increase my earning ability, to increase the quality and quantity of results that I can get for people who are willing to pay me for that increase?" If you focus intensely on results, it will make an extraordinary difference in your life.

Today we are moving away from paper money toward digital money. The great challenge with these new forms of exchange is that people don't actually handle the bills, so they become divorced from realizing how much money they're spending.

I've seen this with my children. They buy things, and they're shocked when the bill comes in. They end up with large credit card bills, and they get notices from people who want payment. The interest starts to rack up, and they're shocked. It takes them two or three years into their twenties before they say, "Whoa!" and pull back. They destroy their credit cards or put limits on them. They pay off the cards every month, and they get back on top of it again.

Of course, the credit card companies have a vested interest in getting people to buy things on credit and discouraging them from thinking of how much they're spending. It's amazing how many people go bankrupt every year as a result of credit card debt.

The major reason for divorce in America, especially among people in their twenties and thirties, is money problems. One or the other is spending money. They say, "It's just a credit card."

They order stuff online, which is another terrible thing, because then you're doubly divorced from the reality. You click the button and place your order, the stuff comes to your door, and a couple weeks later the bill appears. "Who bought this? What happened here? I wasn't really thinking. I just did this."

In debt consolidation, the first thing counselors do is have people tear up their credit cards or consolidate everything into one credit card and put a limit on it so that they can't spend any more in a given month. The credit card is used as merely a convenience. Counselors also have their clients pay for everything in cash. When you pull cash out of your pocket, you realize that this is money you have earned; these are your hourly wages. Suddenly you become crystal clear about how much you're spending, and you stop. Having to pay cash out of your pocket makes you far more thoughtful about expenditures.

Money and time are interchangeable in this way: they can be either spent or invested. If you *spend* money or time, it's gone forever, and you can never get it back. If you *invest* it into something that can pay off in the future, you can benefit from it. The best place to invest your time and money is in increasing your earning ability.

Recently Warren Buffett was asked, "You're the greatest investor in history. Where would you say is the best place to invest today?" He said without hesitating that the best place to invest is yourself—becoming more valuable at earning money.

If you *spend* money or time, it's gone forever.
If you *invest* money or time into something that can
pay off in the future, you can benefit from it for years.

In another study, they asked 1,000 top people, "If you accumulated $100,000, where would be the best place to invest it?" The consensus was to put it back into becoming better at doing what you did to earn the money in the first place.

If you invest in the stock market or real estate, your investment may go up or down. It will be controlled by a hundred factors—by the market, investment experts, competition, and so on. But if you invest in yourself, you own 100 percent of that investment forever. You get 100 percent of the return. You can completely control the investment of your time and money so that you are learning skills that increase your most important results right now. That's the best investment of all. I say this over and over again: the best investment is to increase your earning ability, to become more and more valuable every single day.

One of the great economic laws is supply and demand. If something is in short supply but in great demand, it drives the price up and vice versa. Earl Nightingale summarized this truth many years ago when he said that you'll always be paid in direct proportion to what you do, how well you do it, and the relative ease or difficulty of replacing you. If you are a basketball star, you can negotiate $100 million contracts, because you can hit goals: you can shoot baskets.

In other professions, the people are easily replaced because there are hundreds of thousands of other people who can do the same things. These jobs do not require a lot of mental effort. They allow people to coast, and the great tragedy about coasting is that you can only do it in one direction.

People demand more money even though they've never raised a finger to increase their skill levels so they're worth that money. Yet if the value of your contribution is high, another employer will willingly and immediately pay you more. In fact, employers hire superior staff by finding out who's good at the other companies; then they offer these employees an increase if they'll come and work for them. The fastest way to get a raise is to do your job so well that your employer will pay you to make sure you don't go somewhere else. That's how supply and demand works.

I'll give you an example. During the Great Recession, Citibank received a bailout. Citibank was paying one commodities trader $100 million a year. The executives were brought in front of a congressional committee and asked, "How dare you accept money from the government when you're paying somebody $100 million a year?"

They replied, "This man is the most brilliant commodity trader in the world. He can sense when commodity prices are going to move in a particular direction, and he generates $4 billion a year in income for us. We pay him $100 million, which is about 1/400 of the amount that he generates. That's the deal. If we told him we were paying him too much, we are surrounded by competitors who would hire him away in an instant and pay him the same or more."

Here's a person who is impossible to replace. He has spent his entire life learning the skill of commodity trading. Plus he's probably got an enormous special sensitivity, an intuitive sense that nobody has. Like a star athlete, he puts it all together. You have to do something that is highly valued, and you have to do it better than anybody else. You have to develop a reputation.

In my company, I've always given what I call preemptive increases. A preemptive increase means that nobody has to come and say, "Please, can I have some more money? I've been here for an extra year; I've got more experience. Can I have a raise?" Everybody gets more pay when their value goes up. They don't have to wait a year. If they're doing great work and generating great revenues, we offer them more money, not because they deserve it but because they've earned it. It's just a percentage of the additional value that they're bringing to us. We don't want them to go somewhere else.

If you start a business, nobody will lend you any money, because you don't have any track record. One university professor said to his business students, "When you start your own business, don't use any of your own money. Use only the bank's money. You want to save your own money for your own lifestyle and expenses. So you go to the bank, and you put together an application. You borrow from the bank."

That man is an idiot. I have run businesses for years, and I know the bank will not lend you a penny if you're just starting a new business. Banks are not in the business of risking money. Banks are in the business of making safe loans. You have to prove that this is a safe loan.

When I started my business decades ago, I went to the bank to get a line of credit. They said, "We'd be pleased to give you a line of credit, but it has to be cross-collateralized."

"What do you mean by cross collateral?"

"We want a lien against all of your royalty agreements. We want a lien against your house. We want you to deposit $50,000 in an unmovable account. We want a lien against your car and all your furniture. We want collateral equal to five times the amount we're going to lend you."

"That's outrageous," I said.

They said, "Take it or leave it."

So we took it. That's what you have to do when you start a business. We borrowed a small amount of money. Fortunately, we had good cash flow. We had to go into the credit line every so often, but over time we developed a good rating. All of those cross collateralizations one by one fell away, and now the only thing the bank requires is a personal guaranty.

Some say, "Don't ever give a personal guaranty if you're starting a business." They must be out of their minds. Nobody will even give you a credit card without a personal guaranty.

If you invest in something that pays you a higher return than the cost of the money, that's a good investment. If you invest in things where the money is spent or gone or has exorbitantly high interest rates, as credit cards do, that's *not* a good investment. A good investment is something that yields cash greater than the cost of money. A bad investment is something that consumes cash with no return.

If you invest in a computer that enables you to speed up technological transfers and develop intellectual property so that you can earn money, the computer is a very good investment. It gives you a return that greatly exceeds of the cost and depreciation.

I'm sometimes asked about the relation between wealth and income. Can you have a high income but low wealth?

The joke is that most high-income people are two months away from homelessness because of Parkinson's law. Parkinson's

---

"A good investment is something that yields cash greater than the cost of money. A bad investment is something that consumes cash with no return."

law says that expenses rise to meet income: no matter how much you earn, you spend the same amount and more. The average American lives on about 110 percent of their income. The rest is financed by credit cards, home loans, and so on. They are stretching their means. They don't have cash. Upon retiring, the average American has a net worth of about $41,000, plus Social Security—after forty to forty-five years of living and working in the most affluent economy in history. Why? Because they consider high income to be the equivalent of wealth.

There is only one kind of wealth that really matters. I learned this from an immigrant who became extremely wealthy. He said the only income that matters is money that comes from your money. It's money that is thrown off by your investments. Income is not wealth. Income is merely supporting your lifestyle. The only thing that is wealth is cash flow from other sources. Just remember that: *wealth is cash flow from other sources.* The wealthiest people that I know always talk about cash flow from other sources. When they analyze an investment—and they'll often take six months to do it—they ask, will the cash flow from this investment substantially exceed the cost of the investment and the cost of the money? Also, will it exceed any other alternative use of the money? The smartest people are very careful about investing in order to make sure that the return will be greater than the cost.

If you ask entrepreneurs, successful or struggling, what money means to them, it always comes back to one word: *freedom.* Freedom is the reason for being financially successful. Money means you are free. It means that when you go to a restaurant, you can order without looking at the right-hand column of the menu to see how much it costs.

People love freedom. It is one of the most important, if not *the* most important, of all values. Nobody ever feels they have too much freedom. Some think that others have too much freedom and that laws should be made against them: successful people should be taxed and regulated and punished. But the people who say that feel that they themselves should have all the freedom they want.

Author Barbara De Angelis has this wonderful question: "When will you know that you have enough money, and what will you do then?" Money represents freedom, so we look at how much money you will need to feel completely free. In my business coaching programs, I ask people to determine their number. What is your number? What amount do you need to reach in assets and cash flow, monthly and annually, so that you can stop?

Self-made millionaires spend a good deal of time thinking about the answer to this question: how much will I need in order to be able to support the lifestyle I desire, and what will I do then? They focus on that, and they sacrifice a lot in the short term in order to accumulate the net worth that will yield an amount of income such that they are free. That's the crossover point. At that point, they can get involved in philanthropy and other activities. But for the first part of your life, you must put your whole heart into becoming financially free, and you must do it when you have the highest amount of energy, drive, ambition, and opportunity.

Over the years, I have studied books and articles by and about some of the wealthiest people in history. Sometimes you can read an entire book and get one critical idea. The wealthiest man in history was a German banker named was Jacob Fugger. He was considered to be the richest man in Renaissance

---

Ask yourself: How much money will I need in order to be able to support the lifestyle I desire? And what will I do then?

Europe. He started off with very little, but he was a very good trader, lender, and supporter of ventures, His whole philosophy was frugality, care, caution, precision, sternness, and strictness with regard to money. Similarly, the Rothschilds started off as a small family and became the richest banking family in Europe.

John D. Rockefeller became the richest man in the world at his time. He too focused on frugality, saving, and lowering the price of his commodity, which was oil and gas. People called him a robber baron. Yes, he was a robber baron. He put his competitors out of business. He virtually controlled the entire North American oil and gas market.

The government brought in the trust busters, who broke up his company. But what was Rockefeller's great sin? He continually used economies of scale to lower the cost of gas and oil so that nobody could offer the product at a lower price than he could. Everything he did was to benefit customers, and his competitors considered this to be a terrible thing. So they got together and paid off the government to make laws to break his company up. They broke up Rockefeller's company into five major oil companies, called the Five Sisters. They became the five biggest oil companies in the world. Their competitors still couldn't compete with them, because they kept lowering prices.

If you want to be successful in business, you have to satisfy your customers by providing them with what they want faster, easier, and at lower prices than anybody else. That's one of the greatest financial lessons of all.

One Harvard study concluded that the principal quality of financially successful people is long-term perspective. In today's economy, people are impatient for immediate gratification. It's killing their hopes and dreams. Long-term perspective means that you make decisions in the short term that will have great rewards in the long term: you work hard, save your money, and invest it carefully. You let it accumulate with the miracle of compounding.

Today 65 percent of American adults think that the only way they will be able to retire financially independent is if they win the lottery. Most people think that financial success is a crap game. When they see a Mark Zuckerberg, who became a billionaire in his twenties, they don't understand that he is one of millions of people who have tried to do this. For him, everything came together; the stars all aligned—the advent of the Internet, the advent of rapid data processing, the opening of social media. Everything came together for him at one point in time.

Other people have made billions as well, but they are extraordinarily rare. Most people make their money by working hard, contributing value, saving their money, investing it carefully, and letting it accumulate over time.

Brian Tracy's proven way of Getting Rich:
- Working hard.
- Contributing value.
- Saving your money.
- Investing your money carefully.
- Let it accumulate over time.

TWO

Myths About Money

At this point, we need to clear the deck of the numerous misconceptions, half-truths, and outright lies about the subject—the myths about money.

One reason people stay poor all their lives is that they believe things that are completely impossible. In *Alice in Wonderland*, Alice says to the Mad Hatter, "You can't possibly believe that. It's impossible." The Mad Hatter says, "Sometimes I've believed as many as six impossible things before breakfast." The humorist Josh Billings used to say, "It ain't what a man knows what hurts him, it's what he knows that ain't true." This is fatal to financial success.

The greatest of all laws, which determines everything that happens, was first described by the great philosopher Aristotle 350 years before Christ. He formulated the principle of causality: the law of cause and effect. At a time when everyone believed in gods and miracles and fortune, Aristotle said that we live in an orderly universe, where everything happens for a reason: for every effect, there is a specific cause or causes. If you wish to achieve an effect, you must trace it back to the causes that will bring it about.

If you want to double your income, find somebody who is earning twice as much as you in your field and trace what they did to get there. You will find that everybody who's earning twice as much as you today was at one time earning half as much. So they must have done specific things to achieve these results.

If you ask these people, they'll tell you. If you don't know them personally, read their books, articles, and interviews. They will tell you, because people who earn a lot of money are very generous in telling other people how they did it. If you do what other successful people have done, you get the same result, based on the law of cause and effect.

We live in a world governed by law, not by chance. It's not luck. It's not coincidence. The law of cause and effect says that everything happens for a reason, whether we know what it is or not. There's a cause for every effect. It's a law, and that means that you can control your future.

Every effect—success or failure, wealth or poverty—has a specific cause or causes. Every cause or action has an effect or consequence of some kind or another, whether we can see it or not or whether we like it or not. Sir Isaac Newton, who is considered the greatest physicist in history, called this the *law of action and reaction*. He said that for every action, there is an equal and opposite reaction; this is a law of the universe.

In other words, if you put in value, you get value back—action and reaction. If you don't put in value, you don't get value back. You cannot violate the laws of nature. Napoleon Hill, author of *Think and Grow Rich*, said, never try to violate the laws of nature and expect to win.

The law of cause and effect says that all achievement—wealth, happiness, prosperity, success—is the effect, or result, of specific causes or actions. Earl Nightingale used to say that a person would not sit in front of an empty stove and say, "Give me some heat, and then I'll put in some wood." That's not the way it works. First you put in the wood, and then you get the heat. It would be like the farmer saying to the field, "Give me a crop, and then I'll plant some seed." The world is full of people who say, "If they want me to work harder, they should pay me more." No, you work harder and produce more; then your employer will inevitably pay you more—or someone else will.

**"The Law of Cause and Effect says that all achievement—
wealth, happiness, prosperity, success—is the effect,
or result, of specific causes or actions."**

This law means that if you can be clear about the result you want, you can probably achieve it. You can study others who have accomplished the same goal, and by doing what they did, you can get the same results.

I teach business courses all over the world. They are all based on established, proven principles for building successful businesses. Once I was in Helsinki. A man had been in my seminar the year before. He said he went back and changed his entire business model, and he increased his business fifty times in twelve months. His company went from being a struggling startup to being one of the most successful businesses in the country.

This man was using the law of cause and effect. Certain causes bring about certain effects. The company wan't doing these things before, and they were puzzled why they weren't getting the effects of increased sales and profitability. When you identify these causes and implement them in your life and activities, you'll get the same results that hundreds of thousands of others have gotten.

An interesting point, by the way: In the year 1900, there were 5,000 millionaires in the world. When I started studying this subject in 1980, there were 1 million, most of them in America. By the year 2000, there were 7 million. Today there are 10 million, and the number is growing by about 10–12 percent per year. Millions of people have started from nothing to become millionaires by doing certain things in a certain way.

If only one person had become a millionaire, you could say that was a rare accident. With two, you could say it's a coincidence. But if millions of people from every single background, with every limitation that you could imagine, become millionaires, there are obviously some laws and principles at work. If you can study those who have achieved the same goal, you can get the same results. You can acquire whatever amount of money you really want if you will just do what others have done before to achieve the same results; if you don't, you won't. It's as simple as that.

Nature is blind. Nature doesn't care. It's not as if there is some great power in the universe that wants you to be a big success. Nature is quite neutral. Nature just simply says that if you do what successful people do, you will get the same results, and if you don't, you won't.

I was quite offended when I first heard that, but it's the greatest guarantor of success that there is. You can be a complete jerk, you can be tall or short, or black or white, or educated or uneducated, or a new immigrant or here for generations; it doesn't matter.

The most important expression of this universal law of cause and effect is that thoughts are causes and conditions are effects. To put it another way, thought is creative. Your thoughts are the primary creative forces in your life. You create your entire world by the way you think. All the people and situations in your life have been created by your own thinking. When you change your thinking, you change your life, sometimes in seconds.

The most important principle of personal or business success is simply this: you become what you think about most of the time. This was what Earl Nightingale called his "strangest secret," but it was also said in the Bible: "As a man thinketh in his heart, so is he." It'll be unto you according to your thoughts or your faith. Emerson said the same thing back in the nineteenth century: a person becomes what they think about all day long.

Your outer world reflects your inner world. It's not what happens to you, but how you *think about* what happens to you that determines how you feel and react. It's not the world outside of you that dictates your circumstances or conditions; it's the world inside of you that creates the conditions of your life. The way you think about money and your financial situation largely

---

"You become what you think about, most of the time"
—Earl Nightingale

---

determines your financial conditions. People who come from homes that are well-off are much more likely to become financially successful, because that's what they've grown up with. That's what they've seen around them. That's what they've heard about, so their worldview is that if you work hard and offer value, you can be financially successful as well.

Here's an important point with regard to this principle, and it has to do with one of the major reasons why people fail. It is one of the worst of all vices—envy. Envy and resentment are like twin sisters. They go around together arm in arm. If you envy other people, you resent them. If you resent them, you want to hurt them or bring them down.

There is an entire political philosophy that is aimed at people who envy and resent those who are more successful. But if you do this, you automatically set up a negative force field within yourself. This drives out any chance for you to be successful or happy (unless you do it dishonestly, or you win the lottery). If you envy and resent other people, if you criticize them and pull them down, if you engage in snide, gossipy negative conversations about them, it has no effect on them. They don't even know you're doing it—and frankly they don't care—but it destroys your own hopes and dreams for success.

Never allow yourself to be in a conversation in which people are running down or criticizing successful people. They say, "Oh, yeah, they may be rich, but they're not happy." The rich have been studied at great length, and I can tell you this: they are very happy. They are very happy that their problems are small compared to their opportunities. So always praise successful people, and look up to them with admiration. Learn from them. Speak well about them. Be happy for their success. Then you start to create a force field of energy that draws opportunities to be like them.

People say that your income will be the average income of the five people you associate with most of the time. Whether or not that's true, it's a very good way to think. Your average net worth will be the average net worth of the people you associate with. Why? Because you develop the same thinking styles and attitudes as these people.

Napoleon Hill, author of *Think and Grow Rich*, said the greatest principle of success was the Master Mind. In the Master Mind, you get together on a regular basis with other success-oriented people; you talk over what you've learned, what you've read, what's working for you, and what you've discovered. This Master Mind cross-fertilizes all the minds of those involved, so everybody is thinking positively about each other and about their own possibilities. The Master Mind triggers great wealth. You associate with other people who are at your level or higher, and you start to become like them.

Whatever you believe with feeling becomes your reality. Our greatest challenge is self-limiting beliefs. We believe that we are limited in some way. What held me back for several years was my belief that if you don't get a good education, you'll never be successful.

I bombed out of high school. I didn't pass. I worked at laboring jobs for several years, and I just accepted that I was a laborer. If I lost a laboring job, I went and looked for another laboring job. If I lost a job washing dishes, I got a job washing cars. If I lost my job washing cars, I got a job in construction or janitorial services, or stacking wood in a lumberyard, or putting nuts on bolts in a factory. I just looked for laboring jobs, because

I was told that if you don't get a good education, you won't do well in life.

I accepted that until I got into sales, at the very bottom, and finally started to become successful. I started to make a lot of money, more money even than people around me who had degrees from the best universities. Suddenly I realized I'd been sold a bill of goods.

The starting point of success is to question your self-limiting beliefs. There's a story about the Devil showing a person around hell like a tourist. He shows him all the ways he uses to get people into hell: greed, dishonesty, alcoholism, dope addiction, and criminality.

The Devil takes this man into a special room, which is completely darkened. In the middle is a showcase, like a jeweler's showcase. There's one pinpoint of light, and it shines down on the item inside this glass-enclosed showcase. It looks like a wedge. The Devil says, "This is my favorite of all. This brings more people into hell than any other factor in human life."

The visitor says, "What is it? It looks like a door wedge."

The devil says, "No. This is the wedge of self-doubt. Once I can get this into a person's mind so that they doubt themselves and their abilities to be successful or practice self-discipline, or to work hard and save their money—if I can get them to doubt themselves, then all their strength disappears. Sooner or later they come and join me here in hell for eternity."

Self-doubt is a limiting belief. If you can overcome limiting beliefs, you can change your life. Imagine that there is a belief store. You can go to this store, buy a belief, and put it into your subconscious master program. If you could buy any belief at all, which would be the best one to buy?

**"The starting point of success is to question
your self-limiting beliefs."**

The answer is to buy the belief that you are going to be a
big success in life. Plug that in. Keep repeating to yourself, "No
matter what happens, I am going to be a big success in life."

Look for every trace of evidence to prove this. Someone com-
pliments you for doing something well. You say, "It's true; I'm
on the road to becoming a big success in life." When you read a
book and find a new idea on how to be more successful, say, "Yes,
this is part of my plan. I'm going to be a big success in life."

Insurance magnate W. Clement Stone died worth $800 mil-
lion, which would be several billion dollars today. He started
with nothing, selling papers on the streets of Chicago, with no
father, his mother taking care of him. He taught everybody the
principle of becoming an inverse paranoid. Now a paranoid is
someone who believes that everything is part of a conspiracy to
hurt them and to drag them down. Many people are paranoids.
They are catastrophists. No matter what happens, they think of
the worst outcome that can possibly result. It's very common in
certain upbringings.

Stone said, instead, whenever something goes wrong, imagine that there is a massive conspiracy out there not to hurt you,
but to make you successful. Look at everything that happens
to you and say, "That's good. I wonder what there is about this
that I can use to become more successful. Because I'm going to
be a big success in life."

I learned this many years ago. As soon as my children could
understand English, I began telling them, "By the way, you're

going to be a big success in life." As they grew old, I would continue to tell them, "You're going to be a big success in life."

They would say, "Yes, but how? I don't know; what will I do?"

I said, "Don't worry, you'll try lots of things, but you are going to be a big success in life." I would repeat this over and over, because I know that the influence of parental figures is enormous in young children. You can send them messages that bypass their conscious minds, become permanently logged into their subconscious, and proceed on automatic. I would repeat this statement over and over again.

Now my children have grown up, and they're convinced that they're going to be big successes in life. They work hard. They're honest. They're popular. They're friendly. They're positive. They're never negative. They're never depressed. They're happy and thoroughly engaged in their work and activities. They're doing well because I programmed them at a young age with the message that no matter what happens, they are going to be a big success in life. That overrides and cancels out every temporary failure or difficulty that they have.

If your goal is to be financially successful, believe absolutely that you are going to be a big financial success. Look at everything that happens to you as part of a great conspiracy that's organized by the universe to make you successful. Then you'll say, "Wow! I had this setback; I learned this lesson."

Many young people start a business adventure and go broke, or it fails completely, and they lose all their time and money. This happens over and over again. In retrospect they say, "Thank heavens I went broke, because if that hadn't happened, I might still be struggling with that company. Years might have passed with no success. Now I'm wealthy because of that terrible thing that happened in the past."

That's the key to overcoming this myth that you have limits. The fact is that nobody's better than you, and nobody is smarter than you. Anything that other people have done, you can do as well.

Never compare yourself with billionaires. Compare yourself with other people you went to school with who are doing better than you. This comes out in the most recent research: successful people always compare themselves one up. It's called *social comparison theory*. It's been validated by research at Harvard by Leon Festinger. People compare themselves with upwardly mobile, successful people. No matter what they accomplish, they look at the next step up on the ladder.

The idea is to be like the people who are higher on the ladder instead of trying to tear them down, even mentally or verbally. This has no effect on them, but it destroys your chances for financial success. Be careful what you say and think, because you become what you think about most of the time.

One myth popular today is that you can attract money and wealth into your life using the power of your mind. This is called *the law of attraction*. It goes back 4,000 years, but the people who have written about this law often have only a superficial understanding of it.

The law of attraction says that you are a living magnet: you invariably attract into your life the people, situations, and circumstances that are in harmony with your dominant thoughts. So when you think a thought, remember: you become what you think about.

Myth: The Law of Attraction is attracting money and
wealth into your life using the power of your mind.
Truth: The Law of Attraction will attract the people,
conditions and situations for money and wealth,
but you must then act in harmony with those
dominant thoughts to product money and wealth.

The law of attraction must be considered in combination
with other laws, including the *law of correspondence*, which says
that your outer world reflects your inner world. Wherever you
look, there you are. It's as if you are surrounded by a 360-degree
mirror. Wherever you look, you see yourself. Your predominant
thinking is reflected in the conditions of your life in three major
areas: your health, your companions, and your financial situation.

First of all, your health reflects the way you think about
food, nutrition, diet, and exercise. Why are some people thin
while others are overweight? Thin people think of how they are
likely to feel and look the next day after eating today. Because
they like to feel light and trim and healthy, they are more discriminating in their diet. Overweight people think only about
their pleasure at the moment of eating. They're preoccupied
with how good it feels. Since your appestat—the part of your
brain that regulates appetite—only operates for about twenty or
thirty minutes after the first bite, they eat as fast and as much as
they can until their appestats shut off. As a result, they expand
the size of their stomachs, so they eat more and more. People
who are overweight are gorgers. People who are underweight
are thinking that tomorrow they want to look and feel trim.
You can always tell what a person thinks about most of the time.

The second area has to do with your relationships: you always attract into your life the kind of people that are in harmony with your dominant thoughts. A positive person is surrounded by other positive people.

The final area has to do with your financial condition. You can tell what a person thinks about money by what they're attracting into their lives.

That's the starting point, but there's much more to it than this. Some people have written books that say, all you have to do is think happy thoughts and visualize wealth and success, and you'll attract it, but that's simply not true. The Bible says that faith without works is dead. There's also a proverb that says, pray but move your feet.

In short, you have to work very hard to set up that force field of energy. You cannot set up a permanent force field of energy for financial success if you are not constantly doing things that are in harmony with it.

Another principle is the *law of vibration,* which is known throughout the musical world. Every single substance in the world is in vibration, like a tuning fork. Rocks and stones vibrate; certain plants and animals give off vibrations. Here's an example: imagine a large room with a piano on either side of the room, and you go to one piano and you hit the note of C flat. You walk across the room to the other piano, and the note of C flat will be vibrating in sympathetic harmony with the first one.

This vibration, or sympathetic resonance, is what you see in relationships. The poet Kahlil Gibran wrote about this 100 years ago. He said that when you meet your husband or wife, there will be a moment of meeting, a sympathetic resonance. At this moment, when the eyes meet, this resonance will take place immediately, within seconds. It will take place at that moment, or it will never happen.

People who have been happily married for a long time are asked, how did you meet? Both of them will remember that instant of sympathetic vibration across a crowded room. Their eyes met, and there was a harmony or a vibration that brought them together. They say when you meet your soul mate, you recognize that you've just met your best friend. That's it: there's no drama. There's no trauma. There are no violent ups and downs. It's just there. You just walk away together, and you're together ever after. My wife and I have been married for thirty-six years, and we met in just one moment. We still recall to the instant the second our eyes met. This is part of the law of attraction.

The flip side of the law of attraction, which people don't talk about, is the *law of repulsion*. If you take two magnets and try to push the same poles together, the magnets will push apart. This is a part of many electrical devices. The motor will spin in a certain way, but if the magnets are put in wrong, it won't work at all. Therefore, if you think a negative thought, you will repel out of your life what you want to have. That's why I said you never think negative thoughts about people who are financially successful. You repel all hopes that you could ever have to be financially successful.

Some have negative ideas with regard to money, like "Rich people are bad." These ideas are usually taught to you by your parents when you're young. Often they're poor and angry. But if you believe rich people are bad, you'll never be financially successful, because you'll be sabotaging yourself.

The Law of Repulsion states that if you continually think negative thoughts about what you want, you will repel out of your life what you want to have.

That's why so many people engage in self-sabotage after they make a lot of money. Comic Robin Williams had this funny one-liner: "Cocaine is God's way of telling you you're making too much money." Every so often you have cases where a taxi driver will report that somebody left a briefcase full of money in their cab, or people will lose a large amount of money some other way. It will fall out of their car on the street. These are all subconscious acts of self-sabotage: a person does not believe they deserve their success.

Another important part of the law of attraction is feeling deserving. Almost all problems come from people believing that they do not deserve to have good things happen to them. They work extremely hard on the outside, but inside they have a negative vibration. On the outside, they'll work themselves to death. They'll work sixteen hours a day. Sometimes they'll overdrink; they'll overeat. They'll destroy their marriages and their families. They'll have heart disease and other illnesses. They'll make a lot of money, but then they'll sabotage themselves, because deep down inside they don't believe they deserve it. They've set up the law of repulsion, which takes all the success that they have desperately worked to achieve and drives it out of their lives.

I had a friend who built one of the biggest and most successful businesses in the United States. He came from a very poor background. One day his accountant came to him and said, "You know, if we were to do a couple of little mechanical changes on the cash registers, we could carve off a few cents per transaction, and they would disappear into a separate account."

At the beginning, this man needed the money. But as the business grew and grew, this amount became millions of dollars. He got caught, because the same person who had introduced him to the idea was given a chance to roll or go to prison. So he rolled on his boss, whom he'd sold into the idea. His boss—wealthy, successful beyond imagination, a national legend—was sent to prison for eight years. Because of his poor background, he had this feeling that somehow he didn't deserve it, so he engaged in self-sabotage.

The law of attraction is your thoughts emotionalized. It's like a lamp. You could have a lamp, and it should give off a wonderful light, but not if it's not plugged into electricity. A thought by itself has no emotional context. It's neutral. It's an inert substance. It's only when you multiply the thought times an emotion that the thought starts to have power.

This is why you attract everything you have in your life by the way you think. You can change your life, because you can change the way you think. When you develop a burning desire for financial success and think about it all the time, you set up a force field of positive emotional energy that attracts people, ideas, and opportunities to help you make your goals into realities.

There's a fingerlike part of your brain called the reticular cortex, which is responsible for the reticular activating system. When you emotionalize a thought or a desire, you send a message to that part of your brain, which becomes hypersensitive to anything in your external world that may enable you to bring about that desire.

Say you decide you want a red sports car: you suddenly start to see red sports cars everywhere. You see ads for red sports cars. You see them turning corners two and three blocks away. You see them parked in garages and driveways. It's because you've told your subconscious mind that you are interested in a red sports car. This is part of the law of attraction.

If you decide to take a vacation to Hawaii, you start to see advertisements for vacations. If you decide to lose weight, you see advertisements for weight loss everywhere. This is the way your brain helps you to survive and thrive.

Look at your financial life today and see how it harmonizes with your thinking. Take full credit for all the good things in your life. They are there because you have attracted them to yourself. Also look around at the things you don't like, and take full responsibility for them too. They are there because of you as well, because of some flaw in your own thinking.

What is that flaw, and what are you going to do about it? What are you attracting, or not attracting, into your life? Let's take a very simple example: self-made millionaires. I started researching this many years ago. I was asked by a company if I would give their 800 independent business owners, distributors, a lecture on how to become self-made millionaires. I said, of course.

I hung up the phone and I realized that I was thirty-eight years old. I always wanted to be a self-made millionaire from the time I was a teenager, like everybody else, but I was still broke, still struggling, and still in debt. And I didn't know much about self-made millionaires.

I had two months before I gave this talk, so I sat down and did some research. I began to do some reading. I started off with *The Millionaire Next Door* and *Selling to the Affluent*, both by Thomas Stanley. I started to realize that self-made millionaires are people who have a mindset that attracts wealth. This mindset is a series of ways in which they think most of the time. If you think the way they think most of the time, you start to set up a very high level of vibration. It emanates from you like radio waves and, like a magnet, starts to draw into your life all the things that you need.

When I gave this talk, it was very well received. It was called "The Twenty-One Success Secrets of Self-Made Millionaires." I was asked to give it again and again. I originally gave it in a one-hour form, and then someone said, "Well, we have a ninety-minute slot. Can you give it ninety minutes?" "Yes." "How about half a day?" Eventually I gave it a full day, six to seven hours of delivery with breaks and lunch, because I kept expanding on each of the twenty-one principles.

The most interesting thing happened: within five years, I was a millionaire. The more I taught these principles, the more I thought about them, and the more I practiced them. You become what you think about most of the time. You also become what you teach most of the time. So if you start to teach these principles to someone else, you internalize them at a deeper level. You increase the intensity of vibration. If you teach these principles with conviction, you really feel strongly about them, and you try to make people enthusiastic about them, you start to resonate at a higher level. More and more things start to happen that attract money, and more and more money comes into your life.

Most self-made millionaires come from business, but most of them became millionaires without even realizing it. One

> **Study the mindset of self-made millionaires. If you think the way they think most of the time, you set up a high level of vibration consistent with becoming wealthy.**

year, after several years of work, their accountants told them, "By the way, you're worth more than $1 million now." They said, "Really? How did that happen?" They were so focused on their work and getting paid well for it that they weren't even looking at the accumulation of wealth; it just happened.

That's what happened to me. I sat down because I had to fill out a form to borrow money from the bank, and I had to list all of my assets. I thought, "Oh my God, I'm worth $1.1 million this year." I had to call my wife. This is real net worth. This is what banks consider to be value—home equity, assets in the company, savings accounts, stocks and bonds, and so forth.

The more you study this field, the more you set up this vibration. The more you think clearly, the more you will attract what you think about into your life. For example, if you want to become a millionaire, imagine a check made out to your name for $1 million. Think of the check. Visualize it. Imagine that check made payable to you for $1 million, and put a date on it.

There is a famous story about actor Jim Carrey, who wrote out a check to himself for $10 million for one movie. This was when he was a junior comedian. He had moved down from Toronto to Hollywood, and he would sit up in the Hollywood Hills and look at his check. The check was made out to Jim Carrey: $10 million for one movie. He would look at this check over and over again, and within a few years he was offered $10 million to star in a movie. He said it was exactly the amount that he had written on the check.

Read and feed the picture of your desired into your mind. Every time you do, your subconscious mind takes it like a snapshot, puts it into your permanent subconscious programming, and sees it over and over again.

Another way to visualize success is to see yourself doing the work that you would be doing to earn the money. Many salespeople will visualize themselves selling big products, selling big accounts, closing big deals, whether it's in insurance, ships, planes, stocks, or bonds. They'll see themselves mentally and visualize themselves interacting with customers, seeing the customers smiling and signing the check.

Another way you can do it—and this is what my wife and I did—is to start looking at the kind of home you will live in when you're wealthy. Every Saturday my wife, Barbara, and I would go to open houses in the wealthiest neighborhoods. We'd walk through expensive homes, talking about what we'd like to see in our house. We'd talk about having a staircase, a backyard, a pool, and a gym, and all of those things. Within about three years after doing this, we had moved from a rented house to a beautiful house in a beautiful neighborhood, which we sold. Then we moved from Canada to California, and looked at 150 houses and walked into this house.

We both looked at each other, and we knew this was the house. This was the one we had visualized, written down, and talked about. The owners accepted our offer. Everything fit together neatly, and we've been in that house for decades. As you get older and your kids move away, you think of moving to something smaller, but we don't ever want to move away from this house. They probably will have to carry us out.

In other words, it was exactly the house that we'd envisioned. We had written down forty-two things we wanted in a perfect house. After we'd seen this house, we checked off the checklist. It had all forty-two.

That's how you set up the force field. You pray. In other words, you visualize, get a clear mental picture of what you want, and then move your feet: it's only in moving your feet that you hit the tuning fork and set up the vibration. If you do nothing, nothing happens. Faith without actions is dead.

Get a clear mental picture of what you want—and then move your feet! Faith without actions is dead.

Unfortunately, in all the material about the law of attraction, the word *work* rarely if ever appears. People imagine that you can have something for nothing. This is one of the worst myths of all. It says I can take out more than I put in. But you can only take out a small part of the value that you create. You get a slice of the big, as they say in New York. You get a percentage of the value that you create. You can only take out what you put in, and if you don't put in, you can't take out.

This idea of something for nothing is killing many people all over the world. This misconception is turning people into mental criminals. They're angry at those who have earned money. They demand that money be taken away from the successful and that they themselves should be given money that they do not deserve and have not earned. That's the problem with the idea of something for nothing.

Einstein spent his whole life looking for a unified field theory. This theory would be the one physical principle that would explain everything on earth. Einstein was interested in physics, not humans. I spent almost thirty years looking for a unified field theory of human life. I found it. I call it the *E factor.* This stands for the *expediency factor,* and it says that human beings are neither good nor bad, but always seek the fastest and easiest way to get what they want with little or no concern for secondary consequences.

That explains all the world's problems. It explains criminality. It explains welfare. It explains unemployment. It explains drunkenness, lack of application, laziness. It explains social problems, international problems, dictators, thieves, criminals, marauders.

Throughout history, all wars have been wars of plunder. The first thing the Nazis did in World War II was to plunder the countries they invaded. They stole everything that wasn't nailed down and most things that *were* nailed down. They stole and stole and stole.

Look at every single conqueror. Saddam Hussein had, what, nineteen palaces? While his people were eating dirt, he built billion-dollar palaces. Vladimir Putin is now worth many billions of dollars. It's just pure plunder, something for nothing. It's easy to slip into it, because it's easy to rationalize.

So the desire to get something for nothing, the desire to get something that you have not earned and do not deserve, destroys the hopes and dreams of people worldwide.

The idea that wealthy people think about getting money all the time is incorrect. The most important principle in human life is *service.* Earl Nightingale said that your rewards will always

---

**"Your rewards will always be equal to the value
of your service to others." —Earl Nightingale**

---

be equal to the value of your service to others. The question that you need to ask every day is, what can I do to increase the value of my service to others today?

Go back to the teachings of Jesus and the great prophets. They have to do with serving others, serving the less fortunate. The wonderful thing is that human beings are uniquely designed in our DNA so that our greatest joy comes from serving other people.

I was having dinner with my son and his wife, and they have two little girls. My son's a great father, and my daughter-in-law is a great mother. The little girls are as happy as can be. All the parents think about is doing things for their little girls. Having children and taking care of your children is one of the greatest joys that a person can have. People say, "Kids are terrible at this age." They're never terrible. Having kids and taking care of them gives us so much pleasure that we'll spend our whole lives for them. We'll even put up with a lack of appreciation from them when they grow up. The average man will die eight years younger than the average woman, because he'll work himself to death to provide for his family. Serving his family gives him joy, to the point of being willing to work himself senseless.

Service is critical. Of course wealthy people, successful people, want to earn a lot of money, but money is a way of measuring whether or not you're serving people. It's a way of measuring whether or not what you're doing works, whether it's profitable. Money is the market's way of telling you that this is a valuable expenditure of time and effort. Many people don't understand this. So serving is what people look for. Whenever I'm traveling, I look for products and services that can help people.

John D. Rockefeller started off earning $3.75 a week as a clerk at the bottom of a company. He gave $1.75 a week to charity. That's how he started his life: he gave half of his earnings to charity, and he saved a little bit and accumulated. He was always looking for ways to serve others. People used kerosene lanterns. He was one of the first people to find ways to produce kerosene. When the combustion engine and the automobile came along, his whole focus was on serving people by giving them the products that they needed to enhance their lives at lower prices. He owned everything from the oil fields to the pumps to the pipelines to the railroads to the refineries, all the way through to the gas stations, so that he could keep lowering the price without paying the middleman and serve more and more people at lower and lower prices.

Henry Ford revolutionized the world of manufacturing. When people were doing team manufacturing, it took about 300 hours to make a car, In conjunction with his engineers, Ford developed the production line, which could manufacture cars at such speed that a car could sell for $300 rather than $3,000.

The people actually building the cars, working men, who were at the lowest level of society at that time, could now afford to buy the product they were making. Henry Ford transformed the entire world, and this was his greatest joy. He became one of richest men in the world by making cars available to everybody, which no one had ever done before. Cars had been for the wealthy. Cars were for people who could spend two or three years' worth of the average working man's earnings on them. Now the average person could buy a car. Then somebody came up with the idea of a down payment and payment terms. Now the workingman could buy a car with a small down payment and pay it off over three years. It transformed everything.

Let's look at Sears and Roebuck, which became one of the biggest retailers in history because they came up with the money-back guarantee, no questions asked. Nobody had ever done that in history. They said you couldn't. Sears said, "The people we serve are good people. If we sell them a product through our catalog, they'll only send it back because it wasn't what they thought they ordered; it was the wrong size, the wrong color, or something else. We're going to offer an unconditional guarantee." It turned out that less than 5 percent of people ever asked for their money back. What they asked for was an exchange: 99.9 percent said, "Can I just change it for a different color or a different size?" Sears Roebuck went on to become one of the most profitable retailers in history.

Once I gave at an address at a Walmart convention in St. Louis, with 25,000 people there; I was speaking to 2,000 managers. At one point, the president of Walmart came in, and everybody stopped. He gave a speech. It was about five minutes long. He said, "We at Walmart have a very simple philosophy: we represent people who live from paycheck to paycheck, who have no extra money and who cannot afford to make a buying mistake. Our job is to get them the best selection of products at the lowest possible prices by using our buying power, and then to unconditionally guarantee everything we sell so that nobody ever gets stuck with a product or gets stuck paying more for a product anywhere else. Our job is to help our customers improve the quality and standard of their lives so that they can buy more of the things that they want and need for their family."

He gave that talk with such passion that everybody in the room jumped to their feet cheering, That's the Walmart philosophy: serve our customers. Every thing we do is to get prices down lower and lower so our customers can buy more of the things they need to improve the quality of their lives. Look at Walmart, with 11,000 stores—the most successful retail operation in history. Everybody there is passionate about serving others.

That's how wealthy people think. When they look at a real estate development, a store, a stock, or a product, they're thinking how they can develop a product or service that will help people improve the quality of their lives. That's what they get excited about, and that's what they get rewarded for.

Let me address another myth: it's impossible to reach your financial goals, let alone become wealthy, if you are an employee. Actually, by following a disciplined plan of spending and saving, anyone can become financially free.

Peter Lynch was the most successful investor in history. He built the Magellan investment fund, a multibillion-dollar fund, and then retired wealthy. He said these wonderful words: "It's not timing the market, it's time *in* the market that counts."

If a person buys shares of stock in a mutual fund or index fund, they're becoming owners, because each share of stock represents a percentage of ownership of that company. Ten percent of self-made millionaires are people who worked for another company all of their lives. They worked hard, were paid well, and saved their money. They took advantage of deferred compensation plans—401(k)s and Roths. They put their money away and let it grow.

The reason people don't retire financially independent is that they spend everything that they earn. Then they start to get a little desperate, because they don't have much money saved up at the age of fifty, and they start to try to play makeup ball by throwing whatever money they have or that they can borrow into some get-rich-quick scheme, which inevitably fails. The only ones who get rich from get-rich-quick schemes are those who sell them. So people become desperate.

The fact is that a person who saves $100 a month and invests it in an index fund or a well-managed conservative mutual fund will find that it grows at about 8 to 10 percent per year over time. By saving $100 a month over the course of their working lifetimes, they'll become millionaires.

They say that of 100 people who start work today, one will end up rich, four will be well-off, fifteen will be financially independent, and the other eighty will be either broke, dead, or still working when they reach retirement age.

Some years ago. I was making this point in a seminar. At the break, a mentally and physically challenged young man came up to ask a question. He shouted, "Mr. Tracy! Mr. Tracy! Can I be rich too? I work in a group home, and we

---

Myth: It's impossible to reach your financial goals, let alone become wealthy, if you are an employee.
Truth: Following a disciplined plan of spending and saving, anyone can become financially free.

---

repair furniture. They pay us, and I save $100 every month. If I do that, can I become rich too?"

I had looked at these numbers the day before and had seen that if you saved $100 per month and invested it in a conservative mutual fund for your entire working life, it would be worth more than $1 million when you retired at the age of sixty-five. I repeated those numbers. I said, "Yes, if you were to save $100 a month throughout your career, when you reach the age of sixty-five, you will be a millionaire. You will be wealthier than all the other people driving cars and flying off on vacations. Even with few advantages in life, you will be a millionaire."

Someone who starts early enough, saves long enough, and doesn't touch the money benefits from the miracle of compounding. You don't have to be a company owner. You don't have to be an entrepreneur. You can just invest in stocks and own a small part of many different companies that are well-managed, and you too can become financially independent.

There are three parts to life: your learning years, your earning years, and your yearning years. Your earning years are when you work hard, accumulate money, and put that money to work. Eventually you reach a crossover point where your invested money is earning more than you are. At that point, you can start to gear down, manage your money carefully, and live comfortably for the rest of your life.

Most entrepreneurs have the characteristic of ambition, which is another way of saying that they're hungry, and they're hungry because they came from backgrounds where they didn't have a lot. They say that whatever you felt most deprived of as a child is what you will strive for most as an adult. It's like a defi-

---

Crossover point: **The point where your invested money is earning more than you are earning from your work.**

---

ciency need. It's validated in psychology. These people usually felt that they were deprived of money, so they are hungry to get it. They find that starting a business, selling products, and working hard is the way to get money.

The question is, when is the crossover time? A banker friend of mine said that you can always tell when a business is going to get into trouble: it finally starts to earn a profit, and the owner decides it's time to cut loose. They buy an expensive car, financing it through the bank. They buy an expensive home; they finance it through the bank. You can tell they're going to get into trouble, because they start to spend too soon.

Then, of course, recessions and depressions and ups and downs in industries and in the economy take place. The company takes a dip, the cash flow is cut off, and the person can't make their payments. The car company takes back the car, and the bank takes back the house. This bank always requires a minimum of 20 percent deposit, so they had a very good collateral cushion. If the person could come up with the collateral—which they would do by extracting it from their company—the bank would lend them the money, and they would just take the house back in the next downturn.

My banker friend said the time to start the time to start spending is after you've gone well over the hump: you're financially independent, and you can start investing your excess.

When Warren Buffett came back from college at Columbia University to Omaha, Nebraska, with his wife, he was able to buy a little house. It cost $25,000 or so at the time. He still lives there today. He's the third richest man in the world, according to *Forbes*, but he still lives in that little house; he never went anywhere else. He said it's not a good idea to spend your money too soon, so he got into the habit of investing all of his money and never spending it. Today he's the most successful investor in history.

The critical thing is timing: when you have enough money put aside so that you'd still be capable of making your payments, taking care of your standard of living, and providing for your family even if the whole world went to hell in a handbasket. But if you do it too soon, you'll run the risk of having an unexpected event take place and losing it all.

Another version of the something-for-nothing myth: you can get rich by playing the lottery or winning a jackpot at a casino.

The something-for-nothing disease is like a cancer. It seduces very subtly, and one subtle way is with a dollar for a lottery ticket. Trying to get something for nothing destroys the soul of the individual who does it. It is a cumulative disease. It starts to consume the mental and emotional body.

Recently I was Las Vegas for two days. I stayed in two casinos. I walked back and forth through them for a substantial amount of time, because they're designed that way. You can't get to your room without going through the casinos, past the gaming tables and slot machines. I never spent a quarter in Las Vegas, because, in my philosophy, gambling is fundamentally wrong. It's not because of the amount of money involved. Intelligent people don't gamble, because they know that it's fundamentally wrong.

First of all, nobody ever wins in Las Vegas. If you win, you're photographed and banned from the casinos. It's not even a secret. If you're a professional gambler and you win, they soon photograph you. They sit in what they call "the eye in the sky," and they watch you. If they see you winning money, they can start to check you out against all the other casinos. They check your photograph against those in Atlantic City or Monte Carlo. The casinos all share information.

Nobody wins money in Las Vegas. They only delay the amount that they lose. If you're lucky, you can take longer to lose all your money before you leave. But it still destroys the soul.

I once read a travel article in which the author said, "I have been to hell and back in the last week, and it's a place called Las Vegas in the Nevada desert." He said that he had seen the most miserable, unhappy, unkempt, dirty, smoking, tractor-capped, undershirted people in the world wander through the casinos. He watched overweight men and women gambling away their kids' lunch money. He said, "The looks on their faces are looks of despair, because they've put the money in and can't get it back."

When you check in at a hotel in Las Vegas, they put the entire bill on your credit card, because they know that many customers aren't going to be able to pay when they leave. Friends of mine drove to Las Vegas from LA in a brand-new Cadillac and came back on a Greyhound bus with their suitcases and car gone.

Successful people do not gamble. They will take calculated risks where they can have a major influence on the outcome. They will select a product or service and test it on a small scale. They will make careful investments to see how it works. They will do due diligence to make sure the money that they are putting out has an extremely high possibility of safe return.

Look at the people who do gamble in these casinos. They're always poor people. Poor people gamble disproportionately more than wealthy people. People who can least afford to spend the money are the ones who are doing fantasy football and other sorts of gambling. They cannot afford the money they lose, so it comes out of their children's mouths. These people do not have excess money. It's not like they're making $10,000 a month and their expenses are $5,000, so they've got $5,000 to blow. They're making $2,000 or $3,000 a month, their expenses are $3,500 a month, and they don't have a spare penny. They become desperate.

I've found that gamblers never lose. They always *almost won.* You ask a person, "How did you do in Las Vegas?"

He'll say, "I almost won the big one. I almost won."

"But I see you are taking the bus to work today."

"Yes, I had to leave my car there. I had to get some cash. But I almost won this time. I'll win next time."

Before breakfast, gamblers convince themselves of something that is totally impossible. They get up in the morning and go down believing they're going to win back the money that they lost the night before.

My philosophy is, stay away from something for nothing. When I was young, my mother told me, don't steal. Don't do anything illegal. Don't commit a crime. I never did, and I still don't. I told my kids, never do anything dishonest. Never commit a crime.

I pay my taxes to the penny. I was audited by the IRS some years ago. After seven months of audit, they came back and said,

"The Tracys are the kind of people the IRS really likes. They earn a high income; they pay every single penny of taxes that are required. They have not one single tax dodge or one single questionable deduction. They are completely honest about their taxes. We will never be back."

They've never been back, because they know. They look at our tax returns, which are professionally done, and see that we never mess around with a penny. Like everybody else, we hate taxes, but it's not right to try to get something for nothing, to get money that you have not earned and don't deserve. That's why I'm opposed to gambling of any kind. It destroys the gambler's soul.

Myth: A worthwhile strategy to get rich is by playing the lottery or winning a jackpot at a casino.
Truth: Successful people do not gamble. They take *calculated* risks where they can have a major influence on the outcome.

THREE

Good and Bad Spending

I can still remember my father suggesting that I save 10 percent of my meager little allowance when I was five or six years old. That, to me, was outrageous. I wanted to spend the money on candy. So I would take my allowance, go to the store with my mother, and buy candy. At a very young age I learned to associate getting money with candy, with having fun, with enjoyment, with pleasure. Spending money makes us happy.

As we get older, we have the same feeling. When we get money, the first thing we think is, what can I buy? How can I spend it to make me happy? Tourist resorts are full of trinkets and trash. Streets are lined with stores selling absolute trash, completely useless things. They sell it to people who are on vacation, and part of their vacation is to go up and down the streets, buying trinkets and trash.

If you ask a person what they would you do if they won the lottery, the first thing they talk about is what they're going to buy. You have to change your thinking about spending. Instead of thinking, "If I get money, I'm going to make myself happy by spending it," you have to think, "If I get money, I'm going to make myself happy by saving it."

What do most people do when they get money? I was in a restaurant the other day. It was jammed, which I couldn't understand, because it was Wednesday night. It was payday, and the restaurant was full of people spending because their paychecks had just hit their bank accounts. They were out at an expensive restaurant, spending with both hands. This is because of the association between getting money and spending it.

Eventually we put less and less thought into our spending. Much of spending today is impulse spending. People buy unthinkingly. This is why stores are designed to have impulse purchases at the cash register—things you don't really need or want, seductively displayed.

Time and money can be spent or invested. If you spend it, it's gone forever. If you invest it, you get a return on it. The more time you invest in improving yourself and your earning ability early in your career, the more money you earn, and the more of that money you keep, the more it grows.

There's a law of conservation in money: it's not how much you *make*, but how much you *keep* that determines your financial future. Good spending is where you get a return on your investment: you preserve it, you save it. Bad spending is where the money is gone forever, and you can never recover it.

The Law of Conservation: It's not how much you *make*, but how much you *keep*, that determines your financial future.

At first, you do many things that you don't necessarily want to do—get up in the morning, work hard all day long, study in the evenings, upgrade your skills. You do them for a long time so that for the rest of your life, you can do all the things that you want to do.

Many people try to have their cake and eat it too. They want to have fun, fun, fun, all the time. These people are saying, "Work should be fun, and life should be fun!"

Denis Waitley, the writer and speaker, said that most people spend their lives on things that are tension-relieving rather than on things that are goal-achieving. Albert Gray, a thinker who spent more than twelve years trying to find the secret of success, finally found that it is very simple: successful people make a habit of doing what unsuccessful people don't like to do. What is it that unsuccessful people don't like to do? Well, it's the same thing that *successful* people don't like to do. They don't like to get up early, get started, plan their days, work hard, or upgrade their skills, but they do it because they realize that is the price of success. If you don't sow, you don't reap. If you don't pay the price of success, you will never have it.

There is a great tragedy called *hesitation*, where people *mean* to do something. They're always *going to*, but they hesitate and procrastinate. They never do anything.

If it's possible for everyone to retire financially independent, why don't people do it? First, it never occurs to them. It never occurs to them that they could make a lot of money, because they've never grown up with anybody who is financially independent. They associate with people who spend everything they earn. They think this is the way the world is. They go with the crowd, the herd instinct.

The second thing is, if it *does* occur to them, they put it off. They say, "Well, yes, I could be financially successful, but not now. I'll start in a week, a month, or a year."

The third thing that holds people back is fear of failure. "What if I save my money and I lose it, or what if it doesn't work out?" You avoid that by investing your money very carefully, with experts. Never try to make a big kill or a big score. Always get lots of information.

Sadly, many people also have this fear: "If I set a goal of being financially successful, I'll be criticized by my friends." The answer for this is, don't tell them anything. Keep your plans and your goals to yourself.

Finally, get started. Do the first thing that you need to do: open up a private bank account. Open up a financial freedom account, and put every spare penny you can into this account for as long as you can. The most remarkable things happen.

We know that spending becomes automatic. How do you stop spending? First, you keep track of it. If you go for debt consolidation, the first thing they have you do is to sit down and make a list of every single expenditure, down to the penny. You have to write it all down. You cannot spend, either on a credit card or in cash, without writing it down.

There are some excellent apps to help you track your spending. The very act of taking the time to think through how much you're spending causes you to be more conscious of how much you *are* spending. This often leads you *not* to spend.

My friend David Bach, author of *The Automatic Millionaire*, talked about the latte factor: if you spend $5 on a latte each day and then stop and save that money, that's $25 a week, $100 a month. Accumulated over time, it could make you wealthy.

Another thing that I learned when studying self-made millionaires is that they never buy new cars. They buy two-year-old cars that are in great shape. They have them checked out by a mechanic, and then they drive them forever. Because these cars have lost value through depreciation, you probably can buy a $55,000 car for $35,000.

Once I had dinner with a senior marketing executive at Lexus. He was saying that Lexus had brought in a recertification program. If you lease the car for two years and give it back, Lexus will recertify it with a five-year warranty and resell it. People could then buy that car and drive it forever. That's what I do. I wait till I find a Lexus that's virtually brand-new, because it's been taken such good care of, and get it recertified, which means it's been checked out from bumper to bumper. Then I drive it forever and save.

Let's say you save $10,000 on buying a new car. If you invest that $10,000 in property or a good index fund, over the course of the five or ten years that you drive the car, that money can double and triple. It can turn into a piece of property or a down payment on a piece of property. You may be able to put a down payment on a condo or an apartment and rent that out. The renter pays for all the interest and payments, plus you get a return on your investment. If you start doing that on a regular basis, it becomes quite astonishing. Spending money that continues to grow, investing money that continues to grow— that's good spending. Bad spending is when the money is gone forever.

What should you eliminate from your spending plan if you're serious about building wealth? First, you realize that there are fixed expenses, like rent, cars, and so on. So you live in a smaller place. The Warren Buffett model: he lived in a small house when he was starting off, and he still lives there today. If Warren can do it, you can as well. Live in a smaller place so you can pay lower rent. It has to do Parkinson's law: expenses rise to meet income. When most people have their incomes go up, they move to a bigger place that costs more. Because it's bigger, they buy more furniture, 80 percent of which they never use. Stay in a smaller place, take that additional money, save it, put it away, invest it. Remember: only money that is growing and eventually giving you a return is ever going to be of any value to you.

Back in the eighties I was doing a small real estate development. I saw a notice about a condominium complex where they were selling off the individual units. You could buy a unit for $1,250 down and make monthly payments. I went to look at it: $1,250 was for a $30,000–$35,000 unit. I didn't know anything about investing, but I could come up with $1,250. I think I put it on a credit card.

I bought this little apartment, and then I found out that they were renting the apartments in this complex at about $275 a month. I put mine up for rent in the local paper for $250 a month and immediately got a tenant. It was a single woman with two young children. She paid me $250 a month, and I was paying $275 or $300 a month in payments. I lost money for the first six months, then I raised her rent and broke even. Six months later, I raised her rent another $25.

Soon I got it up to the point where she was paying about $350–$375 a month. She stayed year after year and raised her kids there. They went up through school to college. She stayed there for ten years, and I regularly raised the rent. At a certain point I was getting $1,250 net income back on that apartment.

**To counteract Parkinson's Law when you are starting
out to build wealth (expenses rise to meet your income),
follow the Warren Buffet Model (start off living in
a small house to keep your expenses low).**

And remember: my initial investment was only $1,250! When she announced that her kids had grown up and finished school and that she was going to move out, I sold the apartment.

In retrospect, I think selling it was probably one of the dumbest things that I've ever done. That condo was paying me 100 percent per year in return on my initial investment of $1,250. A 100 percent return. What if I had bought one apartment like that each year? Every time you buy an apartment, the banks will lend you more money to buy more apartments, since you've demonstrated success in this area.

That's one thing that Warren Buffett did. He bought companies that threw off cash flow, and he took that cash flow to buy more companies that also threw off cash flow. Now he's generating $25 billion a year. That's $2 billion a month in cash flow, which he can use, along with more money from the bank. The banks will lend him anything he wants.

If I had done the same thing, I would own apartment buildings, but I was too young to even think about it. Anybody can do that. If you can just find one apartment or condo that's for sale nearby, make sure it's all cleaned up, do a little bit of homework, and make a down payment, you can start your real estate empire.

Earl Nightingale had a rule: invest 3 percent of your income back into yourself, into improving your skills. As soon as I heard

---

Earl Nightingale's Rule: Invest 3 percent of your income in yourself—in improving your skills.

---

that, I began to practice it, and now I say there's no limit on how much you can spend to improve your skills. I took a two-year executive MBA at a university. It cost thousands of dollars, but it was a fantastic investment.

Once a gentleman said to me, "I came to your seminar about eight years ago, and you taught that 3 percent rule: invest 3 percent back in yourself." At the time he was living at home with his mother. He was making $20,000 a year and had an old car.

He said, "Three percent of $20,000 is $600." He bought some books and audio programs and went to one seminar. That year his income went from $20,000 to $30,000. That's a 50 percent increase, which is what I said would happen. And he said he could directly relate this increase to what he learned in those programs.

So now he's making $30,000, and 3 percent of $30,000 is $900. The next year he spent $900, and his income went to $50,000. The following year he spent again—$1,500—and his income went to $80,000. He saw that this really works. He increased it to 5 percent, and that year his income almost doubled. So he decided to go all in. In his fifth year he spent 10 percent of his income, and his income doubled. Then he did it again.

I asked how he was doing now. He said he had passed $1 million that year and he still invested 10 percent back into himself.

"Ten percent: that's $100,000 a year," I said. "How on earth do you do that?"

"It's hard. I used to go to seminars. Now I hire those seminar speakers to come in and spend a day with me coaching. I have special coaches. I have advisors. I travel to international conferences. I have my own learning library, with television sets, videos, DVDs, audios, and books. It's hard to spend $100,000, but my income just keeps going up by 10, 20, 30 percent a year, and these expenses are all tax-deductible."

It really works. *HR* magazine looked at how much return companies nationwide got back on their investment in training. It ranged anywhere from $22 to $33 per dollar that they invested.

Once I spoke to a wealthy woman who said, "I bought one of your audio programs twenty-two years ago. My husband and I listened to it over and over again. We had been married for about three or four years, we had one child, and we started saying, 'I like myself and I can earn a million dollars a year. I earn a million dollars a year.' We started repeating these affirmations, and you know what? Within five years my husband was on Wall Street, making $1 million a year. Because of that one audio program, we became rich."

Many people have increased their income the next year from one book, audio program, or seminar. I have a friend who paid $100,000 to get a personal coach for an entire year and increased their income by a million dollars the following year.

The best investment is to spend on yourself. Spend on making yourself better. What if somebody came to you with an investment and said, "I'd like you to invest in this. It looks like a really good investment. It's got great potential for the future"?

And you looked at it and said, "No, I'm not going to invest in that. I just don't think it has any future. I don't think it's going to be a successful investment, so it would be a waste of my money."

How does this apply to investing in yourself? At an unconscious level, people who do not invest in themselves have feelings of self-doubt and lack of belief in themselves. They've decided that they're not worth it, that investing in themselves is a waste of money, because they have no future.

You can always tell people who have given up on themselves, because they don't invest in themselves. Many people would be shocked to hear that. Yet it is true. Because here's one of the greatest discoveries of all time: you can tell what your beliefs are by looking at what you do—especially what you do when you have a choice. You always choose what is in alignment with your deepest, innermost beliefs and values.

If you're given a choice to buy a latte or buy a CD, to go on a vacation or to attend a seminar, and you choose the fun, you've chosen the tension-relieving activity. You're saying that this is more important to you than your own personal growth and development.

Whatever you do repeatedly becomes a habit. Pretty soon you get into an automatic habit of never investing in yourself. If somebody comes to you and says, "You should get a copy of this boo; it's in paperback now; it's only $12," you'll get angry with that person for suggesting that you move out of your comfort zone. You'll become resistant. You'll actually be negative toward a person who is suggesting that you invest in yourself.

Louise Hay, the spiritual author, once said that the greatest problem of the human race is the feeling "I'm not good enough.

A person who does not invest in him/herself, is evidence of a person who does not believe in him/herself.

It's of no value for me to invest in myself, because I'm not good enough, and it won't do any good because I have no future." You can say, "I've never made that decision." No, but you made it by default. It's like saying, "I never made the decision to be unfit." But if you decide not to exercise, you have made the decision to be unfit by default. If you choose not to engage in developing yourself, you've made a decision to fail at life, because if you're not working on yourself, you have no future.

Another way to think about this is to ask if you were a stock, would you invest in yourself? Would you buy any? That's a shocker too. Do you think you're a growth stock? Are you a stock that widows and orphans could invest in, because your value is going up and up?

Many years ago, I got into financial trouble. I was broke and I needed money. A friend of mine, a very smart guy, said, "I'll lend you some money if you'll give me 20 percent of your profits for the future." My business had no profits at that time, and I said, "Sure, absolutely, no problem." He saw that I was a growth stock, so he gave me $10,000 or $20,000, which I needed to save my business. Then I started to make a profit. My profits were $10,000 and then $20,000 and then $30,000, and I'd give him 20 percent.

Eventually I bought my soul back from him. I gave him $40,000 rather than having him carry interest on my income for the indefinite future. That was the smartest 100 percent return on his money that I had ever given anybody.

Think about that. Are you a growth stock? Are you the kind of stock that makes me say, "I'll invest in you. I'm going to get rich because you're increasing your value so much"?

The number one rule in starting a business is preserve cash. Never buy when you can lease. Never lease when you can rent. Never rent when you can borrow. Never borrow long-term if you can borrow short-term. Therefore, you never lease offices; you rent them, even if you have to move. You buy used furniture. There's used furniture out there for 10 cents on the dollar, and it's fine for now.

Many years ago, I was asked to set up the distribution of a line of Japanese vehicles for western Canada. I found some warehouses in an old district. I bought used furniture, and I set up the offices and parts department. Then my Japanese counterparts came out from Tokyo to look at the facilities. The manager walked in and said, "Aha! Cheap offices. Cheap furniture. I like this. Cheap offices, big profits. We like our distributors to make big profits." He said that he saw distributors who borrowed a lot of money, got brand-new offices, and paid top dollar for first-class everything. They almost all went broke before they made enough profit. "Cheap offices, big profit," he said. I never forgot that. It's a very important lesson, and it was learned by many companies that went broke during the dot-com collapse. These people moved into first-class office premises. They bought first-class everything, and then they ran out of cash.

You want to preserve cash. Never spend it if you possibly can. Save the money. Borrow or rent on a short-term basis. Even get it from your friends if necessary, but preserve cash, because cash is like oxygen to the brain. If you have cash, you can survive. If you run out of cash, the business can turn over

---

**The number one rule when starting a
business is to *preserve cash*.**

---

like a ship in the ocean and sink immediately. A business that's been in business for 100 years can die if it runs out of cash.

Preserve cash. That's what I've learned, because I've made all the same mistakes.

Let me conclude this chapter with three key principles about spending.

First, write everything down. Create a financial plan, and write everything down in detail. Write down what you think things are going to cost, and then double-check. Many companies have gone broke because they underestimated the cost of furniture, raw materials, people, and advertising; they didn't do their due diligence. These words, *due diligence*, have become my favorite words because of the mistakes I've made in business. People make financial commitments and decisions without getting enough information.

Do a thorough financial plan. Committing things to paper forces you to think about them very carefully. Many entrepreneurs hate to create budgets, because they are not detail-oriented people. Then find someone else. Get an accountant, somebody who loves detail, and make a list of everything that you're possibly going to need to do your business. Shop around and double-check to keep your expenses as low as possible.

The second thing is to defer big expenditures as long as possible. If you think you need a whole new computer setup or something like that, put it off for a month or two; it's no emergency. You'll find that people who sell these things will do everything possible to get you to hurry up. If they're paid on commission, they get the commission when the check clears.

In both personal and business finance, you'll find that if you wait thirty days to make any purchasing decision, you probably won't make the purchase. We tend to think, "That's a great idea: a new car or a new computer." If you put thirty days in before the decision, you'll be amazed at how much better your decision is and how rarely you decide to buy the item. I've given myself that thirty-day fuse. At the end, I didn't even remember why I'd been interested in buying those things. Give yourself as much time as possible.

The third thing is to get advice from more experienced people or people who are really careful with money. I have some good friends who are very careful with money. When I ask them about certain expenditures, they have all kinds of great ideas: Don't buy this. Don't buy it here. You can get it cheaper there. You don't really need it. You can borrow here. You can do something else there.

Sometimes you can lease facilities. Jeff Bezos had an overabundance of cloud computing capacity for Amazon, so he began to rent it out. Now he rents out cloud computing capacity to tens of thousands of companies. He's making billions of dollars a year.

If you started your own business, you could just go to Amazon, hook up, and buy everything you need. Also, Amazon will sell things for others, as will eBay, so you don't need to have your own store. You don't even need your own website. Other companies, like Google, will set up websites for you. They'll set up your entire website so that your goods or services can become available to everybody in the world.

These are all ways of putting off expenditures until you absolutely have to make them. You should spend at the point where the savings are so great from making this expenditure that it will more than pay for itself.

Three Rules for Smart Spending:
1. Create a financial plan and write it down in detail.
2. Defer big expenditures as long as possible—at least 30 days.
3. Get advice from more experienced people who are really careful about money.

FOUR

The Ins and Outs of Debt

Because I did not graduate high school, I could only work at laboring jobs. At that point, I had no real problem about debt, because no one would lend me any money. I had no credit cards. I had only enough money in the bank to pay my expenses, and I had to pay for everything with cash.

I worked for several years. I traveled overseas, I visited eighty countries by shank's pony, as it was called: hitchhiking, traveling on buses and trucks, stopping to work here and there to make enough money to go on. Even when I started to make better money in sales, it was pretty much all payable in cash because I was working overseas at that time. I had money in the bank, but never any debt.

Time passed, and I started my own business. I joke that when you start your own business, you learn how to sell again. I sold my house, I sold my car, I sold my furniture, I sold everything I owned, plus I used all of the savings that I had been able to accumulate. I rented a small office, because when you start your own business, unless you're starting with a lot of money, you can go straight off a cliff.

There's a rule that says everything costs twice as much as you expect and takes three times as long to accomplish. If you think you're going to break even in six months, it's going to be twelve months. Everything is going to cost more than you imagined. Even when you make your best budget and gross up by 50–100 percent, you're still going to be surprised.

As a result, I got deeply into debt. I had borrowed some money. I had ordered supplies: printing, mailing, furniture. I thought everything was going great, but I went through all the money, and it was gone. That's when they started ringing my doorbell, phoning me, harassing me, all of that. It was calls, bills, harassers all the time, and I was panicking. We had no money for anything. We were living in a rented house, and I was scrambling the whole time, so I had to retrench.

When you start a new business, lots of people borrow from their friends and relatives; they run up every credit card to the maximum. In my case, I had to borrow against my car and other personal property.

I realized that I was going to have to dig myself out of this debt or go bankrupt. I thought that if I worked really hard, I could do it. The first thing was to go to my bank. It was something like a one-year revolving loan, which had to be paid off. I had borrowed from a bank when I had a house. Now I had no house, but I still owed bank payments.

Then I read that if you keep the loan current with regard to interest, it's not on the books of the bank as a bad loan. They don't have to report it, so they don't have to seize property or

---

**Brian Tracy's Unwritten Rule of Budgeting:
Everything costs twice as much as you expect and
takes three times as long to accomplish.**

---

assets. I went to my bank manager, and said, "Look, I cannot make principal payments, but I can make interest payments on this loan until my business recovers, which it should in the next three to six months."

He said, "As long as you can make interest payments, Brian, then it's not a problem with me, because it appears as a good loan."

Then I went to each of my creditors and said, "Look, I've got this problem: I owe all this money and I cannot pay you off, but I will pay you a small amount each month as a sign of good faith, and I will pay it all off in six to twelve months if you'll just roll with me for a while."

Every one of them, without exception, said, "OK, if you'll make us a good-faith payment every month, we'll roll with you." I owed thousands of dollars, and I'd be paying $50 a month.

I went back to work, and within six months business had turned around. I was able to pay off all of my debts, got all my loans current, and put everything else into shape. It was a terrible one and a half years, but I never went into debt again.

That's why it's nonsense to say, "Don't spend your own money when you start your own business," because to get started, you often have to spend every penny that you can beg, borrow, steal—everything that you own or ever accumulated. According to *Forbes* magazine, 80 percent of new businesses go broke within two years. Every new business is a race against time: do you figure out how to make more money than it's costing you before you run out of money?

Imagine a plane in a dive; it's going faster and faster toward the ground. This is what's happening to your business. You must find a way to pull it out of the dive so that you start to bring in more money than it's costing you. You just barely pull it out of the dive, and then you start to climb again.

The rule in business is, it takes you two years to break even and two more years to pay back the amount of money that you borrowed in the first two years. According to management guru Peter Drucker, no business makes a profit until four years out. If you plan for anything other than that, you're crazy.

I've also been told that it's two, two, and three: two years to break even, two more years to get even with your debts, then three more years to burst into the open sky and start to make a profit. So it's good to have enough money to carry yourself for at least two years, or you'll crash.

When I heard that, I said, "That's nonsense; that's not going to happen to me. I'm different; I'm superior." It took me seven years. It cost twice as much and took three times as long as I thought: two years to break even, two years to pay back the debt, and seven years total to make a profit. Successful entrepreneurs have been through all those phases.

When you see stories about people who have quickly become wealthy in Silicon Valley, it's only happening because of tech-

---

The 2, 2, 3 Rule For Starting a Business:
Two years to break even, two years to get even with
your debts, and three more years to make a profit.

---

nological miracles. We're living through an incredible age, but remember there are 30 million businesses in the United States. Of those, there are probably 100,000 in high-tech. Most of the other 29 million are small to medium-sized businesses, with people trying to sell things and stay alive.

Again, good debt is debt that pays for itself. If you buy products to resell, if you invest in advertising that brings you customers, if you train your staff so they can sell more of your product, if you invest in traveling to meet with clients and you have to put it on a credit card, this is all money that has an expected return on investment. You expect to get back far more than you pay.

Bad debt is where you spend the money, and it's gone forever, like on furniture. When we reorganized our business, we closed our main offices. We opened offices that were much better designed for us. Our employees wanted open space, with modern furniture. Previously I had traditional offices and traditional desk furniture. I'd paid tens of thousands of dollars for beautiful furniture, mahogany desks, all top-notch.

Now it was time to dispense with all of this, and we asked if anybody would like to buy it. They didn't even want it for free. This is what you might call bad debt. In a couple of cases, we had to agree to pay to ship it over to them so they would accept it for free. The whole office was stripped down to nothing, and we didn't make a penny on tens of thousands of dollars' worth of furniture. That's bad debt; there's no return on it.

Like many companies, we also made the mistake of ordering too much product. You think you're going to sell so much. Then you don't, but you still have to pay for the product. You've got thirty- or sixty-day payment plans and a warehouse full of products that are not moving. Many companies go bankrupt because they've stocked too much inventory. That's another example of bad debt.

Why would you do that? Because you can get lower prices if you buy in volume. But it's much better at the beginning to buy smaller quantities, even though you pay higher prices and have lower profit. At least you're not exposed: your cash is not gone, and you don't end up with a warehouse full of dead stock. Dead stock kills businesses, so that's another place where you can get bad debt. If you don't convert your stock into sales very quickly, it can drag your business down. That kind of bad debt is a major reason companies go broke.

As for credit card debt: The credit card industry makes its profit on interest payments, which can run 18–23 percent or even more. There are all kinds of hidden payments, late payment fees, and so on. The only way to use a credit card is to pay if off every month. Credit card debt is the highest-cost debt that you can possibly have, and they make billions of dollars on it. That's one of the worst forms of personal debt.

Extended car loans are another kind of bad debt. Basically you're buying too much car. You should be able to pay off a car in thirty-six months, so if it takes any longer than that, you're buying too much car. Buy less car. Get your ego under control.

Regarding a home equity line of credit—it doesn't cost anything if you don't use it, so they like you to use it. I have a home equity line of credit, but it basically costs $250 a year. A home equity line of credit is a good cushion if you're running a business and they will not give your company a line of credit. You could use a home equity line if you have one. Just make sure

> **Revolving credit card debt (that you don't pay off each month) and extended car loans are examples of bad debt. Pay these debts off as soon as possible.**

that the carrying costs are very low, and read the fine print; those details are important.

I want to touch again on buying furniture on credit cards or credit plans. When I was young and foolish, I went to a furniture store, and they had all these great deals, so I furnished my entire apartment. They had their own financing plan—just sign here, sign there. The interest rate was 24 percent a year. I had no idea that it was almost like Mafia rates, but that's how they made their money. They sold used furniture, and they financed it themselves at 24 percent. You had to make a down payment. I didn't realize that until I started to get the bills. I thought, "Oh my God, if I carry this stuff for three years, I'll end up having paid twice as much," so I paid it all down.

Whenever you get into a financial commitment, take the time to bring the documents home, sit down, and go through them, bit by bit. If you don't understand something, demand a full explanation, because some of these documents are written by geniuses to confuse average people. For instance, with credit cards, it might say 0 percent interest for the first six months, but that's only if you pay off 100 percent each month or if you carry a $2,000 balance. Read the fine print, because you can get trapped. It can say 0 percent or 1 percent per month, or 12 percent per year, and so on.

Be very careful when people call you on the phone and make special offers through your credit cards, your telephone plans, or anything else. These special offers on the phone are usually outrageously priced and include 50–80 percent commission for the people phoning you. They try to get you into stuff you have no need of: extra insurance, extended warranties on cars or technical equipment like computers and cell phones. These can be outrageously expensive and are of no value to you at all.

There are three basic approaches to dealing with debt that you have already incurred. One is called *debt consolidation*. Debt consolidation means putting all your debts together in one company; then you only owe money and make payments to that one company. Although many companies do this, you have to be very careful, because they make big commissions, and a big profit, on consolidating your debt. Almost all people who do this consolidation get into trouble. It can seem as if they've gotten off easy, and as a result they again begin spending beyond their means. This leads to another default and another debt consolidation.

Another way, suggested by financial author Dave Ramsey, is to make a list of everything that you owe and pay off the smallest debt first. It is a good idea, because it gives you psychological momentum to pay off a small debt and cross it off your list, pay off the next debt, and cross that off your list.

Another recommendation I especially like is to pay off the highest-interest debt first. Look at your credit cards: some are charging you 18 percent, some 23 percent, some 30 percent. Pay off the ones that are charging the highest interest first. Dedicate all of your savings to that one. Pay minimum payments on the others just to keep them current. The companies cannot come after you as long as you're making the minimum payments.

Three approaches to paying off debt:
1. Debt consolidation
2. Paying off smallest balance first (Dave Ramsey method)
3. Pay off highest interest balance first (Brian Tracy method)

Once you've decided to get out of debt, there's a series of strategies that you can use. One is to begin saving your money. George Clason's rule is to pay yourself first, which means saving 10 percent or more of your income every month. But if you're deeply in debt, you have to start off small, and there are two ways to do this.

Let's say that you want to save money as well as getting out of debt, but you can't save 10 percent per month. What I recommend is to start saving 1 percent and living on the other 99 percent. People are creatures of habit, so if you can, take 1 percent and save it at the beginning of each month, right off the top of your paycheck. You'll be quite comfortable living on 99 percent. Second month, save 2 percent; third month, save 3 percent.

Over the course of a year, you can build up to saving 12 percent, and the tightening of your standard of living will be so small that you won't even notice it. It may be the equivalent of one latte a day.

When saving money, start with as little as saving 1 percent of your income, and gradually build it up to 12 percent over a year.

Write down everything that you spend, so that you are aware that you're spending this money. Just writing it down will keep you from spending it. Then you save that money. As you begin to save and develop a financial freedom account, your mind space changes, your attitude toward debt changes, and you stop accumulating debt.

It's often recommended that you cut up your credit cards and pay cash for everything. I don't recommend that. It's a bit severe, because it's inconvenient to be getting cash all the time. I only use three credit cards plus a debit card, and I keep everything paid off every single month. If you don't, debt can accumulate—and quickly. I learned the hard way. I carry no credit card debt at all.

As you begin to save 1 percent a month, you'll find yourself spending less and less on debt. It may take you two to three years, but you'll reach the point where you're out of debt completely, and you never get back in. I've spoken to countless people who have done this, and it changes their lives.

Debt causes you to feel inferior, anxious, insecure, and negative. Let's look at the difference between two people. One has money in the bank, and the other is in debt. The person with money in the bank is more confident, more positive, more outspoken. The person who owes money feels a little inferior. They're more cautious; they're more obsequious toward the person who's got money. When you get out of debt, it transforms your personality. Most people who've done it never get back in.

You can do it—just 1 percent a month. If you increase your income, you can save that money instead of spending it and use it to pay down your debt.

There are many schools of thought about carrying a mortgage on your home. If you have a low interest rate, it is much better to carry the mortgage, especially in real estate markets where home prices are going up faster than the payments. Furthermore, a mortgage is an investment, because your house increases in value over the years.

Another strategy is to pay off your mortgage completely or make extra payments. Let's say you get bonuses, sales commissions, or other chunks of cash: you can use those to pay against your mortgage. Some people say if you make two principal payments a month, you can pay off the mortgage in half the time.

That is a good strategy, because it does not cut into your lifestyle, Although it requires a little sacrifice, it takes a thirty-year mortgage down to fifteen years, and then you own the property free and clear.

Today another big topic of debate is college loans. Some look at it as bad debt, others as good debt, because you're investing in yourself for the future.

I was just doing some in-depth reading on the returns on investment for various courses of study. The STEM courses—science, technology, engineering, and math—pay the most. Salaries start at about $76,000 per year when you get out of school, and they go up to about $136,000 a year for petroleum engineers.

Many courses people take are useless, and when they come out, they're unemployable. In the last year, 54 percent of college students were still unemployed one year after graduating from college, because the courses that they took were useless. They're not taking courses that increase their earning ability or enable them to produce results that a company's willing to pay for. So what are they borrowing the money for?

It's like going to Las Vegas. If you're borrowing the money to buy a home there, that's a good investment. If you're borrowing the money to go to the casino, that's not a good investment. People who are borrowing money to take useless courses are making a bad investment, because half of them will be working at minimum wage jobs for the next couple of years.

Eighty percent of college students never work in their field of major after they leave college. They'll never go back to it, because the courses they took are basically entertainment courses. They're excuses to stay at the university, play with your friends, have parties, and drink. That's the difference between good college debt and poor college debt.

A person who borrows to go to medical school or get an engineering degree is very smart, because they're going to be able to pay off the whole thing in a few years. If you don't have a good income because you've got a minimum wage job after taking a useless course of study, that's bad debt. There are some people in their thirties who still cannot buy a house, get credit for a car, start a business, or get a bank loan, because college debt overhangs them like an avalanche.

For the first time in history, the federal government has been insisting that colleges report the amount that their alumni are earning years after graduating in a particular course of study. Those figures become publicly available. The colleges and universities are fighting it screaming and kicking, because they don't want people to know these numbers. Fortunately, if you go online, you can find some very good assessments of how much a person is likely to make with a degree from a particular college.

I just read a study on this, where they looked at the top ten best universities and the worst ten in terms of return on investment. If you go to Harvard and take a degree in law, finance, or economics, your chances of getting a good, high-paying job quickly are very high. Harvard is one of the best. Yale happens to be one of the worst.

If you have a degree from a prestigious university, but it's in useless subjects, it's not going to help you to get a high-paying job. All this information is universally available. You need to do your homework. They show you what the lowest-paying faculties are and what the highest-paying faculties are. It's your job to do some research before you get into debt. It's the same as if you were going to invest in a company: you have to be sure that it's going to have high levels of sales and profitability and will pay dividends to justify the investment.

Some may wonder if it's better to contribute to a 401(k) or some similar account if they have consumer debt. Is it smart to pay off credit card debt while you're contributing to a 401(k)? Or should you just get all the debt paid off before you put one penny in the 401(k)?

Again it depends upon your individual situation—how much you're earning and how much discretionary cash you have. A 401(k) is generally considered to be one of the best investments because it's completely pretax, and it's often matched: if you put in $1, your employer will put in 50 cents or $1. That money can accumulate.

Most people later in life say the biggest regret they have is they did not start putting money into a 401(k) early enough. They should have done it right from the beginning of their careers. They could have ended up financially independent.

Financial freedom expert Dave Ramsey says you should put as much money toward debt as you need to get out of debt completely. Dave's approach requires tremendous self-discipline, which is manifested in delayed gratification. Successful people delay gratification in the short term in order to enjoy financial security in the long term.

Successful people delay gratification in the short-term, in order to enjoy financial security in the long-term.

Dave's approach almost forces you into boot camp. You have to be very disciplined about your finances. Since your habits determine your success, if you're very disciplined about getting out of debt, you're probably going to be a better businessperson, make better decisions, and be more thorough and careful about taking on debt and expenses.

Everything that helps a person to develop self-discipline and delay gratification in the short term builds character, persistence, tenacity, thoroughness, and other superior qualities. It's a really good idea if you can do it, but it's very hard to do. That's why most people don't.

If you're serious, go whole-hog. It's just as if you're going to lose weight: you cut back to 2,000 calories a day, and you stay at that level for one year, without exceptions.

A good friend of mine was overweight. I've known him for thirty years. He'd been about thirty to forty pounds overweight for the whole time. When I saw him recently, he was trim, almost like an athlete. I said, "I've known you all your life; what on earth happened?"

He said he'd gotten one of those calorie counter apps, which tells you you're only allowed 2,000 calories a day. You have to mark down every single food you eat and the number of calories in it. At a certain point the app says, stop: you cannot have any more calories today. If you eat all your calories by noon, you're going to starve until breakfast the next morning. He said you only have to do that a couple of times before you start spreading the calories across the whole day. Final calories are six or seven o'clock in the evening, so you can get to sleep. He said that if you're strict with yourself, it doesn't take long to get into the habit of consuming 2,000 calories. It's the most amazing thing, but you have to be strict with yourself. That's the Dave Ramsey method. Be strict with yourself, and develop the habit of being frugal. If you do this for a year or two, you'll be careful with money for the rest of your life.

When starting a business, many entrepreneurs max out every credit card, go through home equity, and utilize every form of credit available to them. Yet you can be debt-free while starting out in business.

The most important key to success in business is sales. If you can start selling products on consignment, you can launch your business today and generate revenues before you pay anything. There are many websites where you can buy products whole-sale. Then you can develop your own website and sell them, so you don't buy them from the supplier until you have the sale in hand.

The most popular of these is MLM—multilevel marketing, or network marketing. You can start in network marketing with a very small investment for a sample kit. From then on, you take your samples, sell the product, and get the order, then buy the product, deliver it, and make a profit in between. The critical thing is sales ability, so you could start with nothing and sell your way to success.

It's called bootstrapping: you start with your own money, and you grow out of your own profits. It's a slower way to start a business, but it's often the best way, because if you don't have any extra money, you are forced to sell immediately; you are forced to be creative and fall back on hard work and self-discipline. What killed all those dot-com dot-bombs at the beginning of the century was that they had too much money too soon, and they burned through all of it. In fact, I recently read of a company that had raised $400 million in venture capital in Silicon Valley. Before they ever made a sale, they were out of money, and the investors lost it all—$400 million. They had what seemed like a great idea, but they just never got around to selling the product.

Start off by selling the product first. Sometimes you can sell products for another company. You sell for them and make commissions on the sale. You can start your business if you can sell. That's the only way that I know of to do it, and it's a very popular way.

At a certain point, someone may have paid off all their debts, but an unexpected huge expense throws the whole thing off again, so they're back in debt.

You prevent this from happening with the *law of three*. There are three legs to the stool of financial freedom: *savings*, *insurance*, and *investment*. The best way is to go through them one at a time. First is savings. You need between two and six months of normal expenditures put aside so that if you lost your job, you'd be able to continue with your current standard of living for two to six months.

If you have that, you have tremendous confidence in dealing with your world. I've spoken with countless people to whom

---

The three legs to the stool of financial freedom:

1. Leg One: Savings (2 to 6 months of normal living expenses)
2. Leg Two: Insurance (health, automobile, home and life insurance)
3. Leg Three: Investment (401k, Stocks, Real Estate, Your skills, etc.)

I've given this advice, and they followed it. It took them a year to get two months of savings put aside, but they were strict with themselves. Then they got a new boss, or their old boss became a tyrant, or the company began to increase their hours and reduce their pay. They said, "Phooey!" and walked away. They could do it because they had money in the bank, whereas their coworkers had to stay there and take the new negative conditions.

One woman who wrote to me about this matter. She had thought the purpose of her income was to go out and spend it on clothes, cosmetics, and having a good time, but when she heard my advice, she realized that she was trapped. If she didn't have a paycheck every month, she would be desperate. She stopped spending for a year and said it transformed her life.

In short, the first thing you need the equivalent or two to six months of income in savings. Six is best, but at least go for two before anything else.

The second thing you need to do is to insure properly. This is so important. An accountant friend of mine once advised insuring against anything that you can't write a check for, so you get health insurance. I was talking recently to someone who had let go of his health insurance to save money for skiing, but he broke his back while skiing. He was laid up for six months and recuperating for six more months. Letting his health insurance expire set back his whole life.

You need automobile insurance, both collision and liability. You need complete home insurance. If your home burned down, you couldn't write a check for it.

We went to an insurance agency and said, "Here's our life; what do we need?" The agent said, "You need to be insured here; you don't need this much insurance there." They walked us through, and we bought different policies from different agencies, and we've never had a single financial problem.

When you raise four children over thirty years, you have a lot of unexpected reversals, so it's important to have the right insurance. Insure properly. Don't listen to these people that say insurance is gambling against yourself.

You also need life insurance. If you're the primary breadwinner for your family, you need insurance to be able to take care of your family for the indefinite future if something should happen to you. By the way, this gives you a tremendous psychological boost and great piece of mind. It also makes you stronger and more forceful, more positive in the rest of your life to know that your back is completely covered. You are far more confident in taking risks.

I have been deeply in debt, and I know its psychological and emotional implications. Lying awake at night for fear of having your home repossessed, parking your car two blocks away so that it's not repossessed—this is an awful way to live. If it's happened to you, decide to get out of debt, and stay out. Your motto going forward is, "I'm going to live debt-free for life."

Then sit down, make a plan, and move it to the top of your list of priorities. This isn't something you're going to do someday; this is something you're going to do *now*. If you're married, sit down with your spouse and list every single asset that you have, every expense—rent, utilities, gasoline, food—and every debt. Lay it all out on paper.

As I said, you become what you think about most of the time. Self-made millionaires are people like you who at one time decided, "I'm going to become wealthy," and then they did. You never become wealthy without making that decision. If you do and you back it up with action, it's almost impossible for you *not* to become financially independent.

Researchers studied how much time people who are suffering financial problems spend thinking about their money. They think about it twenty-four hours a day. But how much time do they spend actually sitting down, writing out, planning, and thinking about their financial destiny? About one hour a month. This is mostly bill paying time. I've been through this: you sit down and say, "All right, how much are we going to pay on this credit card this month? How much are we going to pay on that bill this month?" You allocate the money until it's gone, and you go back to worrying about money for the next month.

Self-made millionaires spend ten hours a month reading financial publications and thinking about how to organize their financial lives better. As a result, they have a 1,000 percent—ten times—advantage over the person who doesn't.

If you're serious about getting out of debt, even if you're not a detail person, make it a habit to buy a book or magazine on money. Listen to audio programs on money. Make it a top priority to get out of debt and stay out for the rest of your life. If you make that decision, write it down as a goal, make a plan, and put some energy into thinking about it as much as possible, you'll be astonished at how you can transform your financial life.

FIVE

Generating Income

Once you are employing smart spending methods and effective debt management methods, you need to generate strong cash flow, both to invest and to begin living the lifestyle you desire.

Everybody wants to generate a consistently high income that enables them to fund their dreams. Everybody dreams of having money that comes in the mailbox, so that they are earning money and they're not working for it. This is largely a fantasy. I know some people who have had this fantasy for twenty-five years. They're always saying, "This is the one. This is going to be the trick. This is the way that I will start to generate high levels of income without working."

Nevertheless, the only way that you can achieve this goal is by producing products that sell and generate royalties, a commission, a dividend, or some other type of income.

For example, when I started to work to become successful, I started to invest in income-producing real estate. This turned out to be the best investment I ever made, because real estate is solid. It continues to grow in value. Rents and leases from real estate continue to grow with inflation and cost of living increases. Most of the great fortunes are founded on some productive business. The profits are then channeled into income producing real estate or other investments that produce cash flow.

As I mentioned earlier, your work is a commodity that people buy at the lowest possible price for the highest possible quality.

Recently I've done an enormous amount of work in two areas. One is called *business model reinvention*, which is taking a look at your business model. The other is called *personal life model reinvention*, which is taking a look at your personal life model. Both models are revenue generation methodologies: how do you generate profits for a business; how do you generate income for yourself?

The answer is that 90 percent of your income is going to be determined by the quality of the work you do in comparison with that of others who do the same work. Ninety percent of your success in business will be the result of the quality of the product that you offer in comparison with those of your competitors, who are offering a similar product that will do a similar thing. You always have to focus on increasing the quality of your product or service as a company and increasing the quality of your work as an individual.

I'll give you an example. A friend of mine, a very wealthy businessman, needed to have open-heart surgery. He said, "Wow. Even though this is pretty standard today, people do die

---

Ninety percent of your income is going to be determined by the quality of work that you do, in comparison with that of others who do the same work.

---

on the table from open-heart surgery." He began to research the best surgeon in the country for his particular type of surgery. He found this surgeon at the Cleveland Clinic, which is world-famous for having the foremost heart surgery specialists in the world. He contacted him through his doctor, made arrangements, and then flew to Cleveland for his surgery. He spent seven days in the hospital and came back on a private jet. He told me, "If you're going to have open-heart surgery, this is the guy. He's done this surgery more than 5,000 times and has an impeccable success rate. If you need open-heart surgery and you want to be guaranteed that you will recover and have a normal life afterwards, you have to go to this guy."

Of course this doctor is paid a fortune. An open-heart surgeon in a normal city may get something like $50,000; this one gets $250,000. Not only that, he does four procedures a day. It takes about ninety-two minutes to two hours to do an open-heart surgery.

I know this because I subsequently had open-heart surgery with another doctor, also one of the best in the country, who also had done 5,000 surgeries, and who also does between two and four surgeries a day. You only see him once beforehand. The next time you and he cross paths, you are unconscious. He does the surgery, and you never see him again. He's a genius, and he probably gets $150,000 to $250,000 per operation, two to four times a day, because he's in the elite of his field.

I use this example to emphasize my belief that if you're going to invest money, invest it in becoming excellent at what you do. I'm not asking you to win the gold medal in the Olympics or be number one; just be in the top 10 percent, because that's where all the money is. One reason people are not in the top 10 percent in their fields is that they've chosen the wrong field and have no capability for it. But the major reason is, they never decided to be in the top 10 percent. They reached a certain level of competence and then coasted.

One of the most important studies on elite performance has been done by Dr. K. Anders Ericsson at the University of Florida. He says it takes 7,000 to 10,000 hours of hard work over five to seven years to enter into levels of elite performance. He's done most of his work with musicians, but he's looked at other fields as well. Malcolm Gladwell wrote his book *Outliers* citing Ericsson's research. Geoffrey Colvin of *Fortune* wrote *Talent Is Overrated* based on exactly the same idea: you don't have to have talent to start off with, but if you put in the hours, you can develop to the point where you perform at an extraordinary level. As long as it's the right field for you and you put your whole heart into it, you enjoy becoming better and better. You can't become excellent at something that your heart isn't in.

Anyway, Ericsson found that the average person, in the bottom 80 percent, will work to develop competence and confidence in their job; then they will level off and never get any better. The average person—80 percent of the population—is no more productive ten years after they start their first job than they were after one year. It's only the top 20 percent of people who continue to grow.

Gary Becker, a Nobel Prize–winning economist, did an interesting study. He found that the average income of people in the bottom 80 percent goes up about 2 or 3 percent per year as long as they remain employed. This is about the increase in the cost of living, so they never get ahead. The income of the people in the top 20 percent goes up at an average of 11.8 percent per year, because they're continually learning, growing, increasing their skills, and getting better and better in their fields.

So why do some people earn high incomes? It's because they do their jobs very, very well.

I'll give you some great examples. Just think of the chefs who run the top restaurants, like Alain Ducasse, who runs a restaurant in New York. It's one of the most famous restaurants in the world. It's fully booked, and you can pay $500 to $1,000 a night for two people to go there and have dinner.

The top restaurant in the United States is called The French Laundry, and it's located in the Napa Valley, which is very hard to get to. You have to fly into Oakland or San Francisco and then drive an hour and a half to two hours. This restaurant has such high quality that the basic dinner is between $350 and $500, and wine is extra. You can only make a reservation one year out, and they take your credit card and full payment upon reservation. You can't change your mind, change your date, or have a no-show. People fly in from all over the world to go to this restaurant, so that they can experience its chef's gourmet cooking. This is an extreme example of how if you're really good at what you do, people will pay you almost anything.

A lawyer usually earns $200 to $300 an hour. The best lawyers get $2,000 or $3,000 an hour, maybe $10,000. Sometimes they get $100,000, $200,000, or $1 million to handle a particular case, because if you can get this particular lawyer to take your case, it can save you a fortune.

There's only one way to earn a high income: to be so good at what you do that a conscious consumer, wanting the very most for the very least, eagerly pays you premium dollars for your product or service.

All fortunes in America start with the sale of personal services. A person becomes very good at delivering personal services. As a result, people are willing to pay them premiums to hire them, promote them, and give them greater responsibilities. With greater responsibilities comes more money, and with more money comes more opportunity, and so on. But it all loops back to doing what you do in an excellent fashion.

Some employees say they put a lot of time and effort into a company and they should be paid more for that. They say, "I've got twenty years' experience," but the boss says, "Quite honestly, you've only got one year of experience twenty times over," because, remember, the great majority only do their jobs well enough to avoid getting fired and stave off the antagonism of their fellow workers for not doing their share. Once they reach that point, they slip into a comfort zone. They hang out. They chitchat. They go for lunch and coffee. They waste time.

People go to work, and the first thing they do is find somebody to talk to. After they've spoken to that person, they find somebody else to talk to, and then somebody else. They don't start work at 8:30. They find somebody to talk to, and then they say, "Geez, it's eleven o'clock, and I've talked to all my friends about what was on TV, what movies they saw, the family, and the latest news story." Only then do they go to work, and then it's lunchtime. They all go out for lunch, which is usually too long, and then they come back and reestablish their relationship with their friends, talk, talk, talk, and then do a little bit more work. Then they leave because they want to beat the traffic. And they wonder why they don't get promoted. We see this over and over again.

In our company, as I've said, if a person does a really good job, we give preemptive increases. We don't want to lose them, because good people are rare. Good people are the hardest thing to get, and once you get them, pay them whatever it costs to keep them, because a good person costs nothing. A good person contributes far more value than they cost.

The most successful companies are the ones that keep hiring people that contribute more, in either cost savings or revenue increases, than they cost. Each new person actually yields a net profit to the company. That's why companies who have 100,000 employees make billions of dollars a year, because every employee is contributing more than they cost.

This is really the key. A person may say, "I want more money" when they're not earning more for the company. Once I was giving a talk in which I was saying you should set a goal to double your income. One man came up to me at the break—very superior, arrogant—and said, "This might be a nice motivational talk that you're giving, but in my company there's no way they would pay me twice as much. So what you're say-

---

The most successful companies are the ones that keep hiring people that contribute more, either in cost savings or revenue increases, than they cost.

---

ing is really not true. You should make it clearer to the audience that it's a bit of an exaggeration."

"OK," I said, "let me ask you a question. Is there anybody in your company that earns twice as much as you?"

He stopped and said, "Well, yes, of course."

"Are there people that earn three, or four, or five times as much as you?"

"Well, yeah, the senior people, the top people."

"So then," I said, "we can safely conclude that your company is more than willing to pay people three or four or five times what you earn. They're just not willing to pay *you* that amount. Now why would that be?"

He was shocked, as if I'd slapped him in the face, and said, "Maybe it's because I'm not very productive."

"There you go," I said. "It's your fault. *You're* the reason why you're not getting paid more money." He walked away shaking his head.

I call it the survival bonus: "Boss, I didn't die last year, so therefore I'm entitled to more money." No, you're only entitled to more money if you're producing more value. Your share of the extra value you're creating constitutes your increase. No increase in value, no increase in pay.

One of employees' most frequent complaints around the water cooler is that they're not paid what they're worth. They feel that office politics and favoritism keep them from earning a salary commensurate with the value they are delivering.

It boils down to something for nothing: people think they are entitled to more money even though they don't do anything else to achieve it. In the 1950s, something like 50 percent of the work force was unionized. This idea of unionization, which still exists in many government areas and with teachers, is that you get increased pay as long as you don't die. If you have seniority, you're entitled to increased pay. People who have been there longer get paid more. Younger people get less money, even if they're hard-working and competent.

This filters down into a mindset that you should be paid more based on the number of years that you've put in. This is the mindset of people who want more money without earning it, who think they should get more money without creating more value. The fact of the matter is that in every company where people are being paid extremely well, even though they may have started after you, they are contributing more value.

Are you contributing more value now than last week, last month, last year? Are you getting more results that people value and will pay for? Are you contributing more value that, combined with the work of others, your company can use to sell more products and services, generate more sales, and more profitability? If you're not, you haven't earned an automatic increase.

The days of the automatic increase have been gone for almost twenty years, yet people are still standing around the water cooler, wasting time, chatting with their friends, putting in their hours, and complaining that they're not getting paid more.

If you want to get paid more, it's very simple. Start a little earlier. Work a little harder. Stay a little later. One key to success

---

In the modern workplace, you are not paid for the amount of time you put in at the company, you are paid by the value you contribute.

is to work all the time you work. It's always been the key to success. When you go to work, work. Put your head down and work.

Sometimes I'll ask this question. Let's say you've got a job at McDonald's, a minimum wage job making French fries. Many people start their working careers with a job at McDonald's because it teaches them to work, come on time, cooperate, follow instructions, do good work, clean up after themselves, and so on. This is very good training.

You get a job at McDonald's. Could you stroll into McDonald's fifteen or twenty minutes after your shift starts, holding a cup of coffee with your phone in your hand, checking on Facebook, and then hunker down with your friends and shoot the breeze about what you did last night and what you watched on TV, and then take half an hour for coffee and an hour for lunch?

Could you do that if you were working at McDonald's at minimum wage? Absolutely not. You'd have to be there on time, punched in. If you're not punched in, you lose your job. Then you work. You get a ten-minute coffee break in the morning, ten minutes in the afternoon, and thirty minutes at lunch, and you work your whole shift from eight to five.

Everybody knows that; that's what you have to do at a minimum wage job. So how much more important is it if you're a much higher-paid person in a white-collar environment? You're getting paid several times the minimum wage. How can you think you can go to work carrying your latte, showing up late, shooting the breeze, hanging out, reading the paper, checking your email, and not doing any work?

When I make this point at seminars, the audience has a shocked look, because they see themselves. They say, "I couldn't get away with that if I was working at McDonald's, and yet I'm trying to get away with it at work, and I'm wondering why I never get my work done. I'm wondering why I'm behind the eight ball. I'm wondering why I haven't had an increase for three years and not making any progress in my career." It's because you're not working.

Everything comes down to sales. IBM got into serious economic trouble between 1989 and 1991. The stock price dropped 80 percent. They were talking about breaking up the company.

It was a major problem, because in the eighties, IBM was the most respected company in the world. High profits, great leadership, fabulous technology, greatest customer service, ranting raves in all the magazines—*Fortune, Forbes, Business Week.* Two or three years later, it fell out of the sky.

So they fired the president and brought in a new president, Lou Gerstner, who knew nothing about computers. He said, "I don't even know how to turn one on, but I do know about business." He'd started off his career working for McKinsey & Company, one of the best and largest management consulting companies in the world. If they accept the assignment, they come in and fan out. They find the problem, and the solution. They always come in with a solution that works, which is why they're paid so much.

After six months and about $3 million worth of consulting fees, the consultants sat down with the senior people at IBM and said, "We found your problem. It's low sales." They all rolled their eyes and said, "We know that. That's why our stock price is down—low sales, low profits."

The IBM people asked what the solution was. The consultants said, "High sales." Dun & Bradstreet studied the autopsies of tens of thousands of companies that have gone broke over the years, and found that you could put aside all the other explanations—technological, capitalization, competition—it all came down to low sales.

The McKinsey consultants said the solution was very simple: "We've looked at the time usage of your salespeople and sales managers, and we've found that under the previous administration, they were reduced almost to performing as accountants," because the previous administrators had been accountants, who always believe that accounting is the most important function in a business.

Instead of going out and making calls, salespeople were expected to spend 75 percent of their time filling out forms. If they did make a call, they'd have to fill out a five-page sales form. Then the sales managers had to spend all their time reviewing the forms filled out by the salespeople, and nobody was talking to customers.

The consultants said, "Our recommendation is to flip it upside down. People are going to spend less than 25 percent of their time in the office and 75 percent of their time face-to-face with customers. Sales managers are going to spend 75 percent of their time with their salespeople talking to customers."

IBM began the 75 percent rule. They got their salespeople out talking to customers, and the whole company turned around. It went from $1.5 billion in losses to $1.6 billion in profits in one year. The stock went up. Today it's still one of the best-performing stocks in the world.

This rule is now used all over the world in major corporations, because the magic of the IBM turnaround was reported widely. Very simply, get your salespeople and sales managers to spend 75 percent of their time doing sales. If you are a small

---

**The 75 percent Rule: Spend 75 percent of your time
face-to-face with customers, and only 25 percent
of your time in the office.**

---

business, get the owner of the business out there with customers 75 percent of the time. Low sales lead to business problems, and high sales lead to business success.

Recently a study of small to medium-sized business owners was done, and the analysts asked how important marketing, sales, and new customer generation were to their businesses. They all said, "It's the most important thing of all; there's nothing more important than sales and marketing. It's the blood to the brain. It's oxygen. We die without it."

"How much of your time do you, as the company owner, the chief decision maker, spend on sales and marketing?"

"All the time, all day. It's all I ever think about, morning, noon, and night."

The analysts then asked, "Could we come in with time and motion specialists and just walk around, with a note pad and stopwatch, and watch how you use your time on a day-to-day, week-to-week basis?"

"Oh, absolutely, no problem at all."

So the analysts went in and after a month came back with their results: the average business owner spends 11 percent of his or her time in sales and marketing. Everything else is checking on email, social media, chatting with staff, going for lunch, meeting with the banker, and so on.

That's why these businesses were struggling. If you spend 11 percent of your time on sales, the staff will probably spend less than that, because you always set the standard in your company, and everybody follows you.

I've given this advice over and over again. People come back, and they're shocked. Their business, which had been struggling, suddenly transforms into a high-sales, high-profit enterprise, because people are out there selling the product all day long. The rule is, do not do administrative work when there are customers to be seen. When there are customers to be seen, all you do is see customers.

I had a business owner who came to me for one full day of strategy, and we talked about the best use of his time. He considered the best use of his time to be search engine optimization, so that's what he was working on. I asked, "Are you a technical person?"

"No, I'm not a technical person, but it's the key to generating new business for our companies to generate more online leads."

"This may be an important activity," I said, "but it's not *your* important activity. What are the things that you do that generate the most new revenue? What are the activities specifically?"

We went looked over his activities, and he realized that most of his best new business came from recommendations and referrals from his top 20 percent of clients.

"Then," I said, "the best use of your time would be to spend more time face-to-face, or phone-to-phone, with your best clients, making sure that they're happy, offering them additional services, giving them coaching, consulting advice, information."

He said, "You're absolutely right. It's so obvious. The more time I spend with my best clients, the more they buy my services, and the more they bring in their friends, who are at the same level they are. This is going to transform my business."

This businessman had me teach this entire process to everybody in his company. They went from $10 million to $20 million in sales in 2008–09, when the market was tanking. They transformed the business. Their sales went up, and their profits went up even faster, because they were focusing on customers and making sales.

What is the main reason companies fail? One is that they do not aggressively sell the product. There's always an excuse, or they try to run online ads, although there are 36 million people running online ads to sell stuff. They think, "I'll just put some ads on the Internet, and then I'll make a lot of money."

No, in most cases, you're going to have to make direct personal contact. People don't buy products and services. They buy the people, the individuals who sell them, and they buy them because they like them and trust them more than they like other people who offer similar products or services, so you have to focus on this point.

Here's the second reason companies fail: *Forbes* did a study and found that 80–90 percent of business failure occurs because nobody wants the product in the first place. The people selling the product think it's a good product. They even think that other people should buy it. In many cases they themselves don't

---

Two Reasons Companies Fail:
1. They don't aggressively sell the product;
2. Their customers don't want the product in the first place

---

use it, and nobody in their company uses it, but they think it's good for other people.

I was astonished in working with a successful company that sold motivational audio programs, with some with the best motivational speakers, with the best ideas and information. I went throughout the entire company and found that nobody in the company listens to the products. They think these products are good for others, but they never touch them. They never listen to them. They never have them in their cars. They drive around listening to music or talk radio. They never listen to the products that they sell. Surprise, surprise: companies like that eventually go out of business, because, as they say, you have to drink your own Kool-Aid.

I often ask, how many of the people in your company use your product exclusively? It's astonishing—as many as 50–70 percent of people in the company use the competitors' products. They don't use the product that they sell. As a result, when they do offer it, they have no heart. If you use something yourself and you think it's fabulous, you can talk about it with conviction and enthusiasm, but if you don't, you can't.

In short, the main problem is poor sales, and the second is that people just don't want the product or service, and they'll tell you that quite quickly.

Every customer has three choices: they can buy your product, they can buy your competitor's product, or they can buy nothing at all. That's what you have to deal with in every customer contact.

I'm also asked how much salary an entrepreneur should take from the business as a salary. There is no exact answer for that. It depends upon the success of the business. If you're generating high levels of profitability, you can take more income; if you're not, you can't take any.

When I was starting my business, I didn't take any income from it for two years. All I did was generate enough income to keep it alive. I had to sell my house and my car, and borrow from everybody that I knew.

Then I moved my business from Canada to the US and started it again, and eventually staffed it up to twenty people.

Again, I wasn't able to take any income out of my business for about two years. I had to take income from every other source: royalties, books, and audio programs. I even had to borrow to keep the business running, until finally it started to yield profits.

I had to put an enormous amount of money into product development, and product development costs are all up-front. Product *sales* are iffy; maybe they happen in the end. But you have to pay 100 percent for product development, for stocking up your company, before you even get a chance to sell—unless you represent other products. Then you don't have to buy them until you've sold them, so you take the money in between.

It's very common not to take any money out of your business. You scramble for the first couple of years. But let me tell you another interesting point. *Inc.* magazine does a study of the 500 fastest-growing companies every year, and in one recent review, they looked at the founders of these companies.

The fastest-growing company had grown 4,200 times in three years. That's 42,000 percent. Many of the companies had grown fifty or 100 times, which is still phenomenal. Most companies would be happy if they grew 10 percent or 20 percent.

Inc. found two things in common among the founders of these companies. Number one is, they started the company because they loved the product and got excited about it for themselves and their families. Only secondarily did they find that other people loved it as well.

The company that grew 42,000 percent had developed an early education program for children in primary schools, tied into an iPad, where they could help their kids get straight A's. It was a great concept. Every other parent in America said, "I want that. I want my kid to get started off in first, second, third grade with straight A's. That sets them up for life. They have an expectation for life of getting straight A's."

Parents began to storm the company asking for the program. The company grew 42,000 percent, but the founders created it because they wanted to help their kids.

Another entrepreneur, Hamdi Ulukaya, started Chobani yogurt, because he came from Turkey and he really liked Greek yogurt. It was very high-quality, very high in protein, and it wasn't available here. We had this wimpy, milky, watered-down yogurt. Hamdi started to manufacture Greek yogurt at home and sold it to local stores. Even though it cost twice as much as normal yogurt, it started to sell like hotcakes. His story is phenomenal. He borrowed money to buy a bankrupt yogurt factory in upstate New York and manufacture Chobani on a large scale. It's now one of the fastest- and biggest-selling yogurts in North America. My family would never eat anything but Chobani, even though it costs twice as much, because it's so excellent. And remember, he started it because he liked the flavor of Greek yogurt.

When people say, "I want to start a business," I say, "Make sure to offer a product or service that you want for yourself and your family, that you'd sell to your mother, your father, and

---

**"Make sure to offer a product or service that you want
for yourself and your family, and that you would sell
to your mother, your father and your best friends . . ."**
—Brian Tracy

---

your best friends because you think it is so good that it would really make a difference in their lives."

That's the starting point. That doesn't mean that you'll be successful, but without that, chances are, you'll never put your whole heart into the business. You'll be playing golf on Fridays, taking time off, and shooting the breeze, living off whatever you can beg, borrow, and steal until the company goes broke.

Those are the two main reasons companies go broke in the first couple of years: because the product is not wanted, or because it doesn't vigorously sell it.

Experts have studied times of major layoffs in industry downturns like those in aerospace or technology. Many times employees are laid off with a big lump of severance pay, sometimes several hundred thousand dollars. They've been working for ten or twenty years. They've built up their reserves, and they're paid on them.

These people decide, "Doggone it, I'm going to start my own business," which is becoming more and more common. The biggest group, percentagewise, of new business startups is people in their fifties, surprisingly enough, and an even bigger percentage is women. Women are starting businesses more often than men—of all ages.

The first thing that happens to these new business owners is that they are shocked that they have to do everything themselves—answering the phone, emptying the wastebaskets, making the coffee, packing boxes. A large or even medium-sized company has a division of labor. When people start their own businesses, there's nobody else there. Earl Nightingale used to say that the biggest mistake you could ever make is to think that you work for anybody else but yourself. It's only once your business starts to become successful that you can afford to get help.

When I started my business, I had no illusions at all. I got a typewriter, and I typed my own sales letters and letters of agreement with clients. I had to do my own mailing. To get something professionally typed, I'd have to take it to a typist. To get something produced, I'd have to design it or take it to a designer and a printer.

I had been working for a year, flat-out hard work. I designed my own brochures. I made my own sales calls. I brought people into my own seminars. I wrote up the name tags. I delivered the seminar. I served the coffee. I set up the tables and chairs.

I did 100 percent of it myself, with my wife helping me. It was only after a year and a half that I got one-third of a secretary, because I worked with two other guys who were consultant salespeople. We had one secretary, Monica, and we each had one-third of her time. It was only after another six months that my business had grown enough that I was able to hire Monica full-time. So I had my first full-time employee who could do all the little things that I had been doing; then I hired a second, then a third, and so on.

That's how it works when you start a business. Again, if you start a business with too much money and you start hiring too many people, it's astonishing how fast you can go through all your cash. The first thing you have to understand is that you're going to be responsible for everything, especially revenue generation.

I've seen many business owners lose everything. They say, "I will hire a good salesperson." No, you won't. Good salespeople won't work for you, because they're already selling something and making good money at it with an established company, product line, clientele, and reputation.

I remember that I made this mistake. I hired a salesman named Dennis, and he was awful. He had a great story about what a top salesperson he was, but he bled my company dry, promising me roomfuls of customers, piles of sales, checks coming in any minute. I don't think he made a sale in three months. He took a big draw and took commissions on sales that he was supposed to have made. After three months, I confronted him, he walked out, and I never saw him again. I learned that I had to make all the sales myself.

I'm really big on the importance of sales. If you're not a salesperson, you find a partner who is. One of the great partnerships was Hewlett-Packard. Bill Hewlett was tremendous at engineering and developed the first product for the company, which was an oscilloscope. Dave Packard was a fabulous marketer and salesman. This turned out to be one of the great partnerships in business history. Bill and his ever-growing squad of engineers developed fabulous products. Dave and his ever-growing squad of marketing and salespeople went out and sold them all over the world.

So if you're the kind of person who has no sales ability, and if you're not paired with someone who is really good at selling, don't start a business. It's just too dangerous.

Let's go on to investments. The most important thing to realize is that when you make an investment, you are gambling against the knowledge and experience of the person who is selling it. You are believing that it will go up in value. They are believing that it won't, or, worse, that it will go down. That's why every stock exchange is a zero-sum game. The person selling it believes that it's maxed out in value. The person buying it hopes that it's going to go higher.

Income-producing commercial real estate is one of the best foundations for a fortune. But it's not a slam dunk. I have two friends who are full-time experts in commercial real estate, with years of experience. They developed, owned, and operated millions of dollars' worth of office buildings, industrial buildings, and hotels. They went bankrupt when the market went down, because they had mortgages. The mortgages were based on leases, but the tenants went bankrupt. The owners did not have enough money to carry the buildings, which were taken back by the banks and mortgage companies. The owners had to sell their homes and move their families into rented premises. They had to go back on the street to earn a living, although they had been multimillionaires.

People go bankrupt in commercial real estate all the time. Thirty percent of shopping centers in America today are bankrupt or nearly bankrupt, because it's much easier to buy millions of items online. You don't have to get in the car, drive across town, find a parking space, go to a store, and find they don't

---

**Income-producing commercial real estate
is one of the best foundations for a fortune.**

have your size, your color, or what you were looking for. You can just go online and get the exact size, shape, color, at a discount price, delivered to your door the next day. Now shopping centers are being converted into bowling alleys, gyms, or public service operations.

The best investment is something that yields you a steady, consistent, positive cash flow. I've gone into some investments where they will sell you a piece of property yielding no cash flow. You'll buy it at breakeven. It earns you nothing. You have to pay for the mortgage. You have to give personal guarantees, but all you do is break even, because the property is earning just enough to pay the mortgage.

Why? It's because the following year you can raise the rents a little bit, and the following year you can raise the rents a little bit more, like the example of the apartment I mentioned earlier. I bought a property where it was costing me money to service it each month, but I had a tenant, and I gradually increased the rents.

Today I've gone into multimillion-dollar investments where you just break even, but the project is in a growing area, and it is solid. If you hang in there, you're making a slight profit in the third or fourth year. Sometimes it takes seven years before you're actually making a positive cash flow, which pays back the dry years. This is very common in buying commercial property.

Generating income is always risky, because everybody wants high income; everybody wants assured income. As a good friend of mine said speaking to an MBA class, the three factors that you're going to have to deal with throughout your career, which are going to determine everything that happens to you, are competition, competition, and competition.

Everybody wants the good life. Everybody wants to earn good money. Everybody wants a steady cash flow. Everybody wants profits and a good standard of living. So you are surrounded by millions of people who are competing with you to get the same limited amount of cash flow.

I mentioned that Buffett spends 80 percent of his time studying his investments. Carlos Slim, one of the richest men in the world, also spends 80 percent of his time studying investments. That's whom you're going against. You're going against brilliant people with decades of experience, incredible amounts of knowledge, and access to the smartest people in the world, and even they make mistakes 25–30 percent of the time.

If you're going to invest, the best thing is to invest with experts, people with proven track records and a history of making money, and people who have their own money on the line along with yours. The best investments I ever made were with people who put their money in next to mine and who made nothing unless I made money. We made money at exactly the same rate and exactly the same percentage. Those are the best investments of all.

The best investment is something that yields you a steady, consistent, positive cash flow.

SIX

The Creation of Wealth

Most wealthy people don't focus on the acquisition of money: they focus on creating wealth. This is a major distinction, because people assume that money is a thing to be acquired, but in reality it is a means of exchange of value, a by-product of productive activity.

The previous chapters dealt with ideas that, if employed, can lead to a financially free and secure life. But if you desire great wealth—putting you among the top 1 percent—you have to think bigger. You have to either create or add value.

You can distinguish between the *competitive mindset*, where you compete against others to achieve success, and the *creative mindset*, where you add value and create a whole new cate-

---

Most wealthy people don't focus on the *acquisition* of money: they focus on *creating* wealth.

---

gory. Both the competitive and the creative mindsets are very important, but the latter pays much better and is ultimately much more secure.

Most people get rich slowly and by starting off with a single product. You start off with a single product, and you go through a number of stages to make it successful.

If you want to be financially successful and ultimately wealthy, that's a very good and eminently achievable goal. First you say, what would be my product? You define your product in terms of your *value offering*. The value offering is, what difference would this product make in the lives of my customer?

The two critical factors for business success, according to Jim Collins in his book *Good to Great,* are, first of all, you must have a product or service that matters. It must make a difference, it must mean something, it must be something that people want and need and care about. If you have a product that doesn't matter, the only way you can sell it is on the basis of clever advertising and reduced prices. But if you have something that's really important to people, you can charge more, and people will pay more.

The second factor is, the product must be different and superior. Its quality must be so clear that people will choose it over all the similar products that are available. A perfect example is the Apple iPhone. When the Apple iPhone came out, the world leaders in cell phones were Blackberry and Nokia, each of which had 49 percent of the world market. They both dismissed the iPhone as a toy.

But Apple realized that if you could combine all the different things that people wanted to do—send pictures, send messages, download messages, check out restaurants, use applications and so on, plus take photographs and record music—you could create something that nobody else had ever done before. Blackberry and Nokia dismissed it as a toy, saying it was only for teenagers. Nobody was going to want it; there would always be a market for a good, stable, old handset. Five years later, they were bankrupt.

Have you ever gotten in your car and driven a few blocks and realized you left your phone at home? I'll ask 1,000 people this; they'll nod. I'll say, "What did you do?" Everybody says, "Turned around and went back." That is a product that matters. It's so important that if you realize that you're without it, you'll go back and get it.

You have to have a product that matters, a product that makes a difference in people's lives. What job does your product do that people are willing to pay for? What problem does your product solve that is so pressing that people will pay you for the solution? What benefit does your product give that is so important that people will sacrifice in order to own it? What goal does it help them to achieve? What pain does it take away? It's amazing how many products and services are bland. They don't answer these questions, and as a result they fail.

Once you have your product idea, you have to test it with potential customers. You ask, who would be the ideal person for my product idea? Who would buy it the earliest and pay the most for it? Then you go to one or more of these customers and talk to them personally.

This is the revolution that's taking place in marketing today. In the old days, companies would put together a new product and then announce it like a surprise, like the debut of a movie hitting the screens for the first time. Today more and more companies go to potential customers and say, "I think this product would be perfect for you to help you improve the quality of your life or work. What do you think?"

Your customers will give you feedback: "I like this, but I don't like that, and I like this, but I don't like that. If you offered more of this or less of that . . ." Then you go back and adjust the product.

It's like coming up with a new recipe. You have your family taste the dish and ask, "What do you think of this?" "It's too salty or it's too hot or it's too sweet." You go back and tinker with the recipe until everybody says it's great. Now you know you've got it.

That's what's happening today in marketing. It's called *customer cocreation*. When you come up with a product idea and ask how this product can improve an individual's life or work, you go to potential customers and work with them hand in hand until they absolutely agree: "Yes, this is a great product, and I will pay you money to get it." The only thing that really matters is financial transactions: personal acts that give you money. Not only do customers say the product is good, but they will give you money to be first in line. Think of the Apple releases, for which people line up in the streets three days in advance. I ask businesspeople, "How many people do that when you come out with a new product?" And they just laugh. They say, "None, zero, ever."

First, you test the product to make sure that there's a market for it. Then you offer it in limited release and find out how much you can charge for it. Then you start to roll it out and develop a business model that enables you to get the most of your product or service to the greatest number of customers at the best price in the shortest period of time. Then you simply multiply that process and do it over and over again.

That's basically how people start a successful business. Only when you come up with a product or a service that is revolutionary will you make an enormous amount of money. Bill Gates's Microsoft software was revolutionary. It became the de facto software for computers worldwide.

The 4 Steps for Starting a Successful Business

1. Test the product with actual customers to make sure there's a market for it.
2. Offer it in limited release and find out how much you can charge for it.
3. Develop a business model that gets the product to the most customers, at the best price, in the shortest period of time.
4. Repeat and multiply that process."

Bill Gates did not create the Microsoft software. He bought it from someone else who had developed it and then improved it dramatically. He decided to throw his software open to all developers in the world so that anybody could use the code and develop software built on the Microsoft platform. Steve Jobs and Bill Gates both started at the same time, in the early 1980s. Steve Jobs decided to keep the maximum amount of profits possible by closing off the architecture and making it proprietary.

Within ten years, Bill Gates had 90 percent of the market, and Apple was down to 2 percent, even though many people said that Apple's was a superior computer. But Apple had the wrong business model. When they brought out the iPhone in 2006, again they said, "We're going to develop the apps." They developed a few apps, but they were finally convinced that they should open up the architecture and let other people develop them. They admitted that they didn't have the resources to develop a large number of apps. Steve Jobs fought against this for a long time. Finally he agreed to open the architecture to app developers.

That was one of the greatest business decisions in history. It generated billions of dollars and made Apple the richest company in the world. Everything hinged on that one twist in the business model: open the architecture. Bill Gates was already the richest man in the world, because he had opened the architecture at the beginning.

Sometimes you'll take a product or a service and combine it with a unique or different way of marketing that will transform the business. Ray Kroc came up with this idea when he saw the McDonald brothers' hamburger stand in San Bernardino, California. He sold milkshake makers, and this company kept buying more and more milkshake makers. So he went down to see them, and he was amazed. They had a production line producing high-quality hamburgers, French fries, and malts.

Kroc said, "This is a great idea. They have taken this traditional hamburger joint thing and turned it into a machine." People were lined up. Cars were coming from everywhere, and they were making a fortune.

He went to the brothers and said, "Do you want to go into business with me?"

They said, "Sure."

"So we'll start a business; we'll share the ownership"—I think it was 50-50—"and I'll take your entire system back to my head office in Des Plaines, Illinois, and I'll duplicate it."

Kroc wanted to expand, and he went back to the McDonald brothers and told them he had to borrow money and take out mortgages. They said they didn't want to do any of that. They were just a couple of nice guys in San Bernardino, a farming community. He said, "Then let me buy you out." They sold the name and the concept to him for peanuts. The rest is history. The company became successful, and Ray Kroc became one of the richest people.

Entrepreneurs often want to franchise their operations. It takes approximately seven or eight years to sell the first franchise operation. It takes that amount of time to get your business so standardized that it is a guaranteed money machine, working like a Swiss watch, so you can open the doors and see it pump out profits all day.

To prove that you have a system, you simply start another operation. You duplicate the first. You install all the same systems—you make them identical; you don't deviate—to see if the second operation also becomes a money machine. If they become identical money machines, you know you have something. Then you do a third and a fourth. But most people don't reach this point until after the eighth year, because it takes seven years to get all the bugs out of the system. Only then can you duplicate.

One thing to remember: very few business products are franchisable. The product has to be consumable. It has to be something that people buy over and over. It has to have something superior about it compared to all the other, similar products.

Originally Bill Gates was licensing the software for IBM PCs to IBM. But then Microsoft got into financial troubles, as happens in recessions. Gates went to IBM and said, "Look, rather than you paying me a royalty each time you install Microsoft on a PC, why don't you just pay me $350,000, and I'll sell it to you?" They said, "No, we're not in the business of owning software, thank you so much. We have no interest in buying Microsoft for $350,000." Can you imagine that?

Gates had to make the company work, and he did. Today Microsoft could buy and sell IBM before breakfast without even making a blip on their financial statements. I always wonder what great genius at IBM made that decision.

But this was a fluke. Now we look at Bill Gates and say, "Wow, the richest man in the world!" He almost wasn't. Ray Kroc gambled everything too. Peter Drucker said, "Wherever you see a successful business, somebody once took a big chance and won." Self-made billionaires started with nothing and made a billion dollars in their lifetime. They say that the first quality is hard work and self-discipline. The second quality is continuous learning, which we see with Warren Buffett. The third quality is willingness to take a risk: at a certain point they were willing to go all in, like Texas Hold'em, and push all their chips in for one card. They were willing to do that, and the right card came up. That's how you get into the top 1 percent. There is no story of anybody who didn't go all in but still became a billionaire. Of the many people who did go all in, the great majority lost everything and had to start over again.

The top 1 percent versus the other 99 percent: they all start off the same, with the same natural abilities, maybe a good edu-

---

Three Secrets of Self-Made Billionaires:
1. Hard work and self-discipline; 2. Continuous learning;
3. Willingness to take a risk; to go "all in."

---

cation or maybe no. How did these particular people get into the top 1 percent?

It's not the top 1 percent, it's the top 3 percent. The top 3 percent have clear, specific, written goals and plans that they work on, just as an architect designs a beautiful building and continually refines the blueprints. Those in the top 3 percent work on the basis of written goals and plans. These people earn ten times as much as the average, acquire ten times as much, and have much better lives, because they have written goals and plans. So it's not the 1 percent versus the 99 percent. It's the 3 percent versus the 97 percent.

The American Management Association studied this question. They found that the successful people are not necessarily smarter, don't have higher IQs, didn't graduate with better grades, and didn't go to better colleges. They just did certain things differently, and one was that they had written goals and plans. When they started their own businesses, they wrote out clear business plans; then, step by step, they created checklists to find products or services that would work for them.

I worked with some good guys who decided to get into an MLM business. They spent eighteen months going around the country and looked at all the MLM businesses, of which there are hundreds, tried all their products, and finally found one they liked. This one was just perfect for them. They liked the product, and it was ideal in terms of their interests, so they signed on. They had previously gone broke in a business that hadn't worked out. They started again, and this time they became multimillionaires, because they did their homework.

The first time they went into the business, they ran in pell-mell, like dogs chasing cars. This time they sat down and wrote down goals. They said, "What did we learn from the last business? What kind of a product can we sell with pride? What kind of product that people will buy and buy over and over again?" They went through this procedure carefully, then took a look at every product available on their checklist until they finally found one. They experimented with it on a small scale and became huge successes. I know: I spoke with them and worked with them.

To become really wealthy is very rare, but you can dramatically increase the odds in your favor by doing careful planning in advance and thinking it through. As they say, don't lose money. Think it through carefully. Invest time and effort in studying every detail of the business before you put your money in and make an irrevocable commitment.

Author and businessman Michael Gerber speaks of the *system entrepreneur*. This is someone who working on a system so that it can replicate and create greater value, as opposed to the typical entrepreneur, who just works on his or her craft.

As I said, to make a business successful for the first time, as I said, takes seven years. You have to work in that business and put your whole heart into it. Some people came up with an idea of working *on* the business rather than *in* the business, but they had never built a successful business in their lives and still have not. Nobody that ever took advice from them has ever built a successful business either.

I had a good friend who fell in love with the idea of working *on* the business rather than *in* the business. He said, "I followed that advice hook, line, and sinker," he said, "until I was broke. Then I went back to working *in* the business."

Every successful business owner works in the business. There are no exceptions. Look at Bill Gates, one of the most successful businessmen in history. Before he retired, he worked all the time in his business as chief architect officer. He was in there with both hands. He passed on the day-to-day management, the supervision, to the CEO and COO, but he was in his business all the time. From the time he was twelve years old, he was n working intimately with both hands in the business.

I had a management consultant friend who had studied business for over twelve years. He studied hundreds of businesses to find the one quality that made them successful. In his opinion, it was hands-on management. These owners do their rounds, like a doctor checking patients in the hospital. They take the pulse, they look at the eyes, the mouth, the face, the blood pressure. The doctor's got his hands on the patient the whole time. Starting a business is like an emergency situation. If you go to an emergency room, you'll find the doctors and nurses are right there. They've got their hands on the patients all the time, because this is the critical moment.

I was reading a poster on the wall of a hospital some time ago, which said that with stroke, the first thirty minutes determine whether or not this person will live or function afterward: you've got to move fast. Here are the symptoms of a stroke; here's what to do immediately; here's where to go.

It's the same when you start a business. It's always red alert time. Every day is an exciting day, because it can make or break your business. If you have an accumulation of bad days, with no money coming in, no profits, no sales, you go underwater.

You have to have your hands on the business to make it successful. Anybody who says that you don't has never had a successful business. If you want to be successful, you've got to put your whole heart into it. You can increase your odds of success, but you can never guarantee them.

In creating wealth, we are talking about a different mindset than the one we hear about in the media. The media assume that there is a fixed pie of resources, for which we all compete. We might call this the scarcity mentality, whereas the abundance mentality teaches that money is not divided but created.

For most of human history, wealth was usually transferred through plunder. People owned estates they had taken by plunder. The villagers were required to turn over a portion of their crops to the people who owned the land, who in turn took those crops and sold them. That was their major source of revenue.

The barons lived in fabulous castles and had fabulous lives. They would march out with jewels beyond belief when the average person was eating dirt and having to pay 10 percent or 20 percent of their earnings in tribute. This is what led to Robin Hood and similar legends Europe.

Ayn Rand talked about the development of capitalism over the past 200 years. She said that for the first time in human history, the expression *making money* was used. Making money meant that you could bring together resources, raw materials, labor, and machinery to create wealth where none had existed before.

A good friend of mine, who's now one of the richest men in the world, wrote a book in which he said that man's material welfare, MMW, is the equivalent of tools times time or money. Man's material welfare comes from tools, which cost an enormous amount of money to develop, multiplied by labor. This has never really changed.

Today, to create one job in retail costs $100,000, and to create one job in petrochemical engineering costs $500,000. To create a job in any industry requires an investment of a certain amount of money by someone who has saved it from expenditure. Capitalism is really "savings-ism": wherever there are high levels of savings, there are high levels of capital available to be invested in new businesses and opportunities, which can create wealth and jobs.

Creating wealth means finding new ways to serve other people. You're finding ways to enhance their lives and work such that they will eagerly pay you for your product or service. At the same time, you have to compete, because everybody else wants the same customers; they also want to create wealth and enjoy the same standards of living.

The abundance mentality says there are unlimited opportunities, because human beings have unlimited wants. This is one of the most important principles I've ever learned. As long as there are human wants unfulfilled, human problems unsolved, and human needs that have not been taken care of, there will always be opportunities for the creative minority.

Mark Zuckerberg came up with the idea of Facebook (now called Meta) in his dorm room. Harvard freshmen are given a

---

The *abundance mentality* says there are unlimited opportunities, because human beings unlimited wants.

---

book containing pictures of all their classmates so that they will get to know each other. They call it the Facebook.

Zuckerberg simply turned this idea into a website. People could check the faces of people at Harvard. It was a great idea. More people started to do it. Originally, they wouldn't make any money at all; it was just a project for the geeks. Pretty soon everybody at Harvard was on it, because if you wanted to be socially active, if you wanted people to know about you and what you were interested in, you would go onto this site. People started to share messages back and forth. It was so successful that someone from Yale said, "Can you do a Yale Facebook?" They said, "Sure." They took the same technology and used it to create another Facebook.

Then they realized that people who aren't at college would like this as well. Facebook grew by accident. Everybody wanted to be able to communicate online with other people and share stories and pictures. It was very primitive at the beginning, and it was just a fluke of luck that they happened to develop a technology that went viral. Imagine: there are billions of people on it now. It was a real stroke of luck, because before Facebook there had been other social media sites, Myspace for example, but they disappeared.

Warren Buffett took a course at Columbia from a man named Ben Graham, the father of value investing. He said that you have to look deeply into the fundamentals of a company to find out if the product or service that it sells really generates value for the customer. This is called *value creation* and *value capture*. Value creation has to do with the customers: the product enhances their lives greatly in excess of the amount of money they pay. Value capture is capturing part of the value that you create for other people.

Graham taught this philosophy of looking at businesses in terms of their underlying value and how some companies offered better or different value than their competitors. Simultaneously he asked, who were the people in the company? Were they good managers? Were they astute developers of new products? Were they ambitious and always looking for ways to improve the product?

Warren Buffett grew up in a nice family. His father was stationed in Washington, and when Warren was about fourteen years old, they didn't have much money, so he got a job delivering newspapers in the morning. He got one penny for every newspaper he delivered. He was careful with his money, and his parents paid all of his expenses. For the next two years he delivered more than 200,000 newspapers, getting up at four in the morning, delivering papers, coming home, going to school.

He saved $2,000, graduated from Columbia, and with his $2,000 he started his business. He followed Ben Graham's idea: invest in companies that are valuable. These companies offer products and services that people like and want and which are considered superior to competitors' products, and which generate profits. Then he would use those profits to buy other companies that are also selling similar products or services that people want and are generating profits. Then he would take that larger profit stream and repeat the process. He kept doing that to the point where today he's the most successful investor in history.

It's a very simple concept. Ben Graham gave Buffett the this concept of how to invest, and he never deviated from that idea. All over America and the world, there are now *Buffett billionaires.* These were people, doctors, lawyers, salespeople, business owners in Omaha that knew Warren. He was a nice young guy in his twenties, starting off investing his own $2,000, and did pretty well. So they said, "Warren, would you invest my money as well?" He said, "Sure." You never hear of these people, but some of them are worth $5 billion and $6 billion, because they got in with Warren when he was a young guy investing money.

Another example is Sara Blakely, who invented Spanx. She had the same concern that many women have: they want to look good. She found that there were many kinds of undergarments for women, but none were using the plasticized technology that would make them look firm. That's how she started Spanx. She developed her own models and had them manufactured. Then she went from store to store to get the stores and boutiques to sell them on consignment. Finally, people started to buy her products, and the business started to take off. At the beginning she had to work extremely hard to get stores to carry the product, but it turned out to be the right product at the right time.

Sara Blakely is a smart businesswoman. She got good designers, and she still designs every product herself. As a result, the company went ballistic, because there are so many people who wanted the product, and she had such a great quality product. Today Spanx is the best. It's considered the highest-quality product.

It's the same with Apple iPhones. People will pay much more for an iPhone than for a Samsung or some other phone, because the iPhone is considered to be the premium product in the market. There's always a huge market for the premium product.

The most important principle of wealth creation has to do with continuous improvement. The greatest enemy of success in every area is complacency, the lure of the comfort zone. Many companies come out of the gate with a great product. The product receives tremendous acclaim, they sell a large quantity of it, and the competitors pile in. It's an economic principle: wherever there are higher-than-average potential profits, competitors will rush in with similar products or services to get a piece of those extra profits.

Many years ago, I wrote a newspaper article entitled "The Only Cure for High Prices Is High Prices." People always complain when prices go up. Don't worry, because competitors will rush into the market to create much more of the product. There will be an oversupply, and then the prices will drop. They'll crash, because people will be trying to move their overstocks. The higher the price, the faster competitors come in, the more they produce, and the lower the eventual price.

There's a formula: CANI, which stands for *continuous and never-ending improvement.* This is why some companies and individuals are incredibly successful. Every day in every way I'm getting better and better. I'm learning more. I never go to sleep at night without knowing more than I knew when I got up in the morning. Successful individuals are always listening to audio programs, reading, and upgrading their skills.

The CANI Formula = Continuous and Never-Ending Improvement.

My business partner attended a high-level workshop on digital marketing and was very excited. Some of the smartest people in the country shared concepts in digital marketing that increase response rates, sales rates, and repurchase rates. He is always going to these courses, and he's built one of the most successful digital online marketing businesses in the country.

It's no miracle. Continuous and never-ending improvement enables companies to make their products faster, better, cheaper, easier, and more convenient. If you keep pushing forward, constantly looking for ways to improve, you're going to hit a Spanx or a Facebook or a Microsoft—something that nobody has ever seen before. It's because you're way out in front, taking risks, pushing the outer edge of the envelope, always looking for ways to make your product better and better. If you're really fortunate, you can break through. That's how people become billionaires within one generation.

SEVEN

The Laws of Money

One of your major goals in life should be financial independence. You must aim to reach the point where you have enough money so that you never have to worry about it again. The good news is that financial independence is easier to achieve today than it has ever been before. We live in the richest country at the richest time in human history, irrespective of short-term economic ups and downs. We're surrounded by more wealth and affluence than ever before.

As I said, when I started off there were a million millionaires and a few billionaires. Now there are 10 million millionaires and 2,000 billionaires. The billionaires are increasing at the rate of forty or fifty a year, which is an incredible amount of money. One thousand million dollars, starting from nothing! Your goal should be to participate fully in what many people are starting to refer to as the golden age of mankind.

Money has an energy of its own, and it's attracted to people who treat it well. Money tends to flow toward those people who can use it to produce valuable goods and services and create employment and opportunities that benefit others. At the same time, money flows away from those who use it poorly or spend it in nonproductive ways. Your job is to acquire as much money as you honestly can and use it to enhance the quality of your life and the lives of those you care about.

Money has an energy of its own, and it's attracted to people who treat it well—those who use it to produce value and not spend it non-productively.

The first law of money is the *law of cause and effect,* which says that everything happens for a reason; there is a cause for every effect. This is the iron law of human destiny. It says that we live in a world governed by law, not by chance. Every effect, success or failure, wealth or poverty, has a specific cause or causes, whether we know what they are or not.

This law means that all achievement, wealth, happiness, prosperity, and success are the direct and indirect effects or results of specific causes or actions. If you can be clear about the effect or result you want, you can probably achieve it. You can study others who have accomplished the same goal, and by doing what they did, you can get the same results.

The law of cause and effect applies to money as much as to any other subject. Financial success is an effect. As such, it proceeds from certain specific causes. When you identify these causes and implement them, you will get the same effects that millions of others have gotten. You can acquire whatever amount of money you want if you do what others have done before you to achieve the same results. If you don't, you won't. It's as simple as that.

Your ultimate financial goal should be to accumulate capital until your investments are paying you more than you can earn on your job. This is your basic goal in life. The sooner you set this goal and work on it, the sooner you're going to achieve it.

The next law is the *law of investing*. It says, investigate before you invest. This is one of the most important of all the laws of money. You should spend at least as much time studying a particular investment as you do earning that money to begin with. Never let yourself be rushed into parting with money. You have worked too hard to earn it and taken too long to accumulate it.

Investigate every aspect of the investment well before you make any commitment. Ask for full and complete disclosure of every detail. Demand honest, accurate, and adequate information on every investment. If you have any doubt or misgivings, you will probably be better off keeping your money in the bank or ia money market account than risking the loss.

The first corollary of the law of investing is that the only thing easy about money is losing it. It's hard to make money in a competitive market, but losing it is one of the easiest things you can do. A Japanese proverb says making money is like digging with a nail, while losing money is like pouring water on the sand.

The second corollary of this law comes from the self-made multibillionaire Marvin Davis, who was asked about his rules for making money in a *Forbes* interview. He said he has one simple principle: *don't lose money*. If there's a possibility that you will lose your money, don't part with it in the first place. This principle is so important that you should write it down and put it where you can see it. Read it and reread it over and over.

Think of your money as a piece of your life. You have to exchange a certain number of hours, weeks, and even years of your time to generate a certain amount of money for savings or investment. That time is irreplaceable. It's a part of your precious life that is gone forever. If all you do is to hold on to the money rather than losing it, that alone can assure you financial security. Don't lose money.

The third corollary of the law of investing says that if you think you can afford to lose a little, you're going to end up losing a lot. You remember the old saying: a fool and his money are soon parted. Another saying says that when a man with experience meets a man with money, the man with the money is going to end up with the experience, and the man with the experience is going to end up with the money.

Always ask yourself, what would happen if you lost 100 percent of a prospective investment? Could you handle that? If you couldn't, don't make the investment in the first place.

This issue comes up with the current cryptocurrency craze. Cryptocurrency has recently seen such wild variations in value that it can only be considered an extremely speculative investment. The fact that many cryptocurrencies are held by a small number of investors, who can undercut prices to bring the value down and buy the coin back to make it rise again, reaping enormous profits, is only one element of the risk.

Although some major financial institutions are going into crypto, it is not viable as a conservative investment strategy. If you feel you just can't miss out on its possibilities, the most prudent approach is what is called *hodling*. Originally a typo for

> ## The 100 Percent Rule: If you can't handle losing 100 percent of a prospective investment, don't make the investment in the first place.

holding, the term caught on as a crypto strategy: "hold on for dear life." That is, you buy the coin as a long-term investment and hold it through its ups and downs in the belief that its value will continue to rise in the long run. But this is by no means a proven strategy. The principles above apply here: do exhaustive research before taking any action, and even then, only invest in crypto what you can afford to lose entirely.

The fourth corollary of the law of investing says, *only invest with experts who have a proven track record of success with their own money.* Your aim is to invest only with people who have such a successful track record with money that your risk is dramatically diminished. Again, don't lose money. If ever you feel tempted, refer back to this rule and resolve to hold on to what you have.

Invest only in things that you fully understand and believe in. Take investment advice only from people who are financially successful as a result of taking their own advice. When the market turns down, many people who offer financial advice are broke, homeless, unemployed, and working at McDonald's. Many of those who sell financial success or get-rich-quick products have no other money than what that they get from selling these products to unsuspecting people.

The next law is the *law of compound interest.* This says that investing your money carefully and allowing it to grow at compound interest will eventually make you rich. Compound interest is considered to be one of the great miracles of all of human history and economics. Albert Einstein described it as the most powerful force in our society, if not in the universe. When you let money accumulate at compound interest over a long enough period of time, it increases more than you could imagine.

You can use the rule of 72 to determine how long it would take for your money to double at any rate of interest. You simply divide the interest rate into the number 72. For example, if you are receiving 8 percent interest on your investment, you divide the number 72 by 8, getting the number 9. This means that it would take you 9 years to double your money at 8 percent interest. It's been estimated that $1 invested at 3 percent interest at the time of Christ would be worth half the money in the world today. If the money had been allowed to grow and double and double again and again, it would be worth trillions.

In short, the key to compound interest is to put the money away and never touch it. Once you begin accumulating money and it begins to grow, never touch it or spend it for any reason. If you do, you lose the power of compound interest. Even though you spend only a small amount today, you'll be giving up what could be an enormous amount later on.

If you start early enough, invest consistently enough, never draw on your funds, and rely on the miracle of compound interest, it will make you rich. An average person earning an average income who invested $100 per month from age twenty-one to age sixty-five and who earned a compounded rate of interest of 10 percent over that time would retire with a net worth of $1,118,000.

Begin a regular monthly investment account and commit yourself to investing a fixed amount for the next five, ten, or even twenty years. Select a family of mutual funds and invest-

---

If you start early enough, invest consistently enough, never draw on your funds, and rely on the miracle of compound interest, it will make you rich.

---

ment instruments. Keep your money working month after month and year after year.

The next law of money is the *law of accumulation.* This says that every great financial achievement is an accumulation of hundreds of small efforts and sacrifices that no one ever sees or appreciates. The achievement of financial independence will require a tremendous number of small efforts on your part. To begin the process of accumulation, you must be disciplined and persistent. You must keep at it for a long, long time. Initially you will see very little change or difference, but gradually your efforts will begin to bear fruit. You will begin to pull ahead of your peers. Your finances will improve, and your debts will disappear. Your bank account will grow, and your whole life will improve.

The first corollary of the law of accumulation says that as your savings accumulate, you develop a momentum that moves you more rapidly towards your financial goals. It's hard to get started on a program of financial accumulation, but once you do, you find it easier and easier to keep at it. The *momentum principle* is one of the great success secrets: it takes tremendous energy to get started and overcome the initial resistance to financial accumulation, but once you have started, it takes much less energy to keep moving.

The second corollary of the law of accumulation says, by the yard it's hard, but inch by inch anything's a cinch. When you first begin thinking about saving 10 or 20 percent of your income, you'll immediately think of all kinds of reasons why it's not possible. You may be up to your neck in debt; you may be spending every single penny that you earn just to keep afloat.

If you find yourself in this situation, there's a solution. Begin saving just 1 percent of your income in a special account, which you refuse to touch. Begin putting your change into a large jar every evening when you come home. When the jar is full, take it to the bank and add it to your savings account. Whenever you get an extra sum of money—from selling something, a repaid debt, an unexpected bonus—instead of spending it, put it into your special account. These small amounts will begin to add up at a rate that will surprise you. As you become comfortable with saving 1 percent, increase it to 2 percent, then 3 percent, then 4 percent, and 5 percent, and so on. Within a year you'll find yourself getting out of debt and saving 10 percent to 15 percent, even 20 percent of your income without really affecting your lifestyle.

The next law of money is called the *law of magnetism*. This says that the more money you save and accumulate, the more money you attract into your life. The law of magnetism, often called the *law of attraction,* has been a primary reason for wealth building throughout history. This law explains much of the success and failure in every area of life, especially financially. Money goes where it is loved and respected. The more positive emotions you associate with your money, the more opportunities you will attract to acquire even more.

The first corollary of the law of magnetism is that a prosperity consciousness attracts money like iron filings to a magnet. This is why it is so important for you to start accumulating money, no matter what your situation. Put just a few coins into a piggy bank. Begin saving even a small amount of money. That money, magnetized by your emotions of desire and hope, will begin to attract more to you faster than you could imagine.

The second corollary of this law says it takes money to make money. As you begin accumulating money, you begin to attract more money, and more opportunities to earn money, into your life. This is why it's so important to start even with a small amount. You'll be amazed at what starts to happen. Take time every day, every week, and every month to reflect on your financial situation and look for ways to deploy your finances more intelligently.

As I said before, self-made millionaires think about financial accumulation ten times as much as poor people. Every week they take time to think about how much they have, how it's deployed, how they can earn more, and how they can invest it better. The more time you take to think intelligently about your finances, the better decisions you will make and the more money you will have to think about. And the more you think about your savings and investments, the more you will attract into your life.

Another law is called the *law of accelerating acceleration.* This says that the faster you move toward financial freedom, the faster it moves toward you, from a variety of different directions.

Everyone who is financially successful today has had the experience of working extremely hard, sometimes for years, before they got their first real opportunity, but after that, more and more opportunities flowed to them from all directions. The major problem most successful people have is in sorting out the opportunities that seem to come at them from everywhere. It will be the same for you.

Look at the companies in Silicon Valley who invested millions and then tens of millions and then hundreds of millions. They invested in companies like Facebook and Google and Apple, and they made billions of dollars. Now opportunities come to them like rivers from all directions to invest in places where they'll make billions more.

Peter Lynch, former manager of the Fidelity Magellan Fund, one of the most successful mutual funds in history, said that the best investments he ever made were those that took a long time to come to fruition. He would often buy the stock of a company that did not increase in value for several years. Then it would take off and go up ten or twenty times in price. This strategy of picking stocks for the long term, the Warren Buffett strategy, eventually made Lynch one of the most successful and highest-paid money managers in America.

This brings us to the *law of the stock market*. The value of a company's stock today is the total anticipated cash flow of that company discounted to the present day. This means that a share of stock represents a share of the ownership of the company. It entitles the owner of the share to all the benefits and risks of ownership, including profits, losses, stock increases, declines in value, good or poor management, and increasing or decreasing demands for the products or services sold by the company. When you buy a share of stock, you are an owner of everything that takes place in that company. You are investing a certain sum of money and betting that your return will be in excess of what you could earn in a guaranteed investment such as a bond or a money market fund.

Purchasing a stock is a form of gambling, because both the future of the company and the value of the stock are unpredictable. They are determined by countless market forces, such as sales, competition, technological change, interest rates, quality of management, world events, weather, and many other factors.

The first corollary of the law of the stock market is that bulls make money, and bears make money, but pigs get slaughtered. People who invest aggressively when the market is rising make money. People who sell short and protect themselves when the market is declining also make money. But greedy people who try to make a killing in the market almost always lose money.

More than 70 percent of day traders or flash traders today—people who move in and out of the market completely one day or sometimes one hour at a time—lose money. Many of them lose everything.

The second corollary is that long-term investing in the American stock market is the best way to achieve long-term financial security. The value of stocks traded on the US markets has increased an average of 11 percent over the past eighty years. As a result, a person who began investing at the age of twenty and who invested $100 per month in a mutual fund that increased an average of 10 percent per year would retire with a net worth of more than $1 million.

The third corollary is that dollar cost averaging over the long run will make you rich. Market timing doesn't work. It is virtually impossible for you or anyone to consistently buy stocks

---

Market timing doesn't work. It's *dollar cost averaging* over the long-term, that will make you rich.

when the prices are low and sell them when the prices are high. It's always better to buy the stocks of a good, solid company selling valued and respected products and services and hold on to those stocks for the long run. This is value investing, and it's what makes people in the stock market wealthy.

Corollary number four says the stock market is managed and made by professionals. Every purchase of a stock represents the sale of that same stock by someone else. The person purchasing the stock is betting that the stock will increase in price. The person selling the stock is betting that the stock will decline in price. Every stock purchase and sale is therefore a zero-sum game, with one person betting his wisdom and judgment against that of another.

Most of these people are professionals who do this for fifty to sixty hours each week, sometimes for several decades. This means that your safest course of action is to invest in an index fund, which represents all of the stocks in a given index and goes up or down based on the average trend of the entire market. The most popular type of index fund is the Standard & Poor's 500. These index funds have consistently outperformed more than 80 percent of professionally managed mutual funds over the years.

The next law of investing is the *law of real estate*: the value of a piece of real estate is the future earning power of that particular property. The value of any piece of property is determined by the income that it can generate when it is developed to its highest and best use from this moment onward. A piece of property may have sentimental value to a particular owner, but its dollar value is directly related to its future earning power.

Millions of acres of land will never have any value, like desert land, which has no future earning power. It cannot be developed to produce income, provide accommodation, or satisfy any human needs. There are vast areas in many large cities where property values are declining. For instance, think about Detroit, where growth and development have come and gone and will probably not return. Every day men and women are selling homes and properties at less than they paid for them or are losing them to foreclosure, because these properties have declined in earning power, in rental power, and therefore in value.

The first corollary of the law of real estate is that you make your money when you buy and you realize it when you sell. This is very important. Purchasing a piece of property at the right price and under the right terms enables you to sell it at a profit. Many people think that they'll make their money when they sell the property, irrespective of how they purchased it or at what price. This is putting the cart before the horse. The more carefully you investigate a piece of property and the more thoroughly you prepare a purchase offer, the more likely you are to be able to sell that property at a profit later on.

The second corollary of the law of real estate is, the three keys to real estate selection are location, location, location. Each piece of property is unique: there's only one property like that on earth. Your ability to choose a property in an excellent location will have more of an impact on its future earning power than almost any other decision that you make.

The third corollary of the law of real estate is that real estate values are largely determined by general economic activity in the area and by the number of jobs and the level of wages. This is very important when you're selecting a neighborhood or a community in which to invest. Generally speaking, the value of property increases at three times the rate of population growth and two times the rate of inflation. When you purchase property in a fast-growing community, you are virtually ensured of above-average increases in value.

For example, Silicon Valley, in Santa Clara County, California, has seen a incredible explosion of employment and high-tech, high-paying businesses. Consequently, real estate values have increased five and ten times over what they were a few years ago.

The most important factors affecting the value of real estate in any area are the level of new business formation and economic growth in the surrounding area. Decide today to purchase a piece of real estate for investment purposes. The only way you can learn about real estate investing is by actually becoming an owner of a property and using your knowledge and skills to increase its value.

At the beginning of the twentieth century, a man named Bernard Baruch started off as a stock market runner, running orders back and forth from stockbrokers. While most of his friends were playing around, he would ask the people that he was delivering orders to why they were making those decisions. Over time, he got a sense for what made a good stock market investment, and he began to invest a dollar a week. Within a few years, he was one of the richest men in America. He was an advisor to six presidents. He wrote books and articles. At the end of his life, he summarized what he called the ten rules for investment success, and I'll finish off this chapter with them.

1. Don't speculate unless you can make it a full-time job. Every decision you make is a bet against the decision of someone else who is studying the stock market forty, fifty, or sixty hours a week.

2. Beware of anyone bringing gifts of inside information or tips. The number one way to lose money in the stock market is to act on tips from people who don't know what they are talking about, like taxi drivers, bartenders, barbers, and even close friends at work.

3. Before you buy a security, find out everything you can about the company, its management and competitors, its earnings and possibilities for growth. Be patient, disciplined, objective, and unemotional. Take the time to investigate before you invest.

4. Don't try to buy at the bottom and sell at the top. This can't be done (except by liars). When you buy a stock, decide at what price you will sell it; when it hits that price, don't be greedy. With program and computer trading today, you can set a sell price on a stock that will be triggered automatically when it hits that price. You will never go broke taking a profit.

5. Learn how to take your losses quickly and cleanly. Don't expect to be right all the time. If you have made a mistake and you see that the stock is going down, sell it and cut your losses as quickly as possible.

6. Don't buy too many different securities. Better to have only a few investments which you can watch than to have too many. Diversification spreads your risk, but it also eliminates any chance you might have for major gains if one of your stocks were to increase rapidly in value. This

is a rule for people who are going to trade in the stock market, not for the average person, who is much better off buying an index fund and just holding it.

7. Make a periodic reappraisal of all your investments, and see whether changing developments have altered their prospects. Use zero-base thinking. Always ask when you have new information, "If I had not already made this investment, knowing what I now know, would I purchase it again today?" If the answer is no, that is your cue to sell.

8. Study your tax position to know when you can sell to greatest advantage. Be aware of the capital gains taxes that apply to your transactions. Remember that the only thing that counts is the amount that you have left after taxes. The timing of stock market purchases and sales to create capital gains and capital losses is an area with which you should be thoroughly familiar.

9. Always keep a good part of your capital in a cash reserve. Never invest all your funds. If you keep a cash cushion at all times, you will also be in a position to take advantage of unexpected opportunities that come along. You will also have an emergency reserve to act as a buffer no matter what happens in the marketplace.

10. Don't try to be a jack of all investments. Stick to the field you know best. Warren Buffett said he never invested in dot-com or Internet stocks "because I just don't understand them or how they're valued." He never lost money, while everybody else lost a fortune when the dot-com dot-bomb explosion took place. Usually the most successful investors concentrate on becoming knowledgeable about

the companies in one particular industry. Pick an industry that interests you so that you'll enjoy keeping current with it.

Remember, the key to success in investing is to investigate before you invest. Invest carefully. Get all the information that you require. If you're going to be an active investor, you have to watch your money all the time. If you're not going to be an active investor, the best thing that you can do is buy an index fund that has a low cost of management and which will grow as the market moves. You can put it aside, sleep well at night, and never worry.

A Review of The Laws of Money

- **The Law of Cause and Effect:** Everything happens for a reason; there is a cause for every effect.
- **The Law of Investing:** Investigate before you invest.
- **The Law of Compound Interest:** Investing your money carefully, and allowing it to grow with the interest compounding year after year, will eventually make you rich.
- **The Law of Accumulation:** Every great financial achievement is an accumulation of hundreds of small efforts and sacrifices that no one sees or appreciates.
- **The Law of Magnetism:** The more money you save and accumulate, the more money you attract into your life.

- The Law of Accelerating Acceleration: The faster you move toward financial freedom, the faster it moves toward you—from a variety of directions.
- The Law of the Stock Market: The value of a company's stock today is the total anticipated cash flow of that company discounted to the present day.
- The Law of Real Estate: The value of a piece of real estate is the future earning power of that particular property. "

EIGHT

How to Protect Your Wealth

Once you have become financially successful and acquired a good level of wealth, your job is not over. You need to install various forms of wealth protection so that you don't quickly lose what it took years to build.

One of the worst mistakes is the walk-on-water syndrome. We make a lot of money by becoming very good in our own field. We think, "I'm so good that I can transfer that knowledge, ability, skill, or confidence to some other area and do equally well in that area."

When the real estate market was booming back in the 2000s, somebody approached me and said, "There's tremendous opportunity to build self-storage units in fast-growing communities, because they fill up like rain barrels in the springtime. They cast off a very high level of cash flow, they increase in value, so all will be well."

So I said, "Sure, why not? Sounds like a good idea." This man had some good contacts, he was doing a lot of work, and had put together some financial proposals. It sounded very good, so I began to invest—a little bit in the beginning, then more and more, until I invested about $20 million in self-storage. It wasn't all my money, but it was all leveraged off of investments that I made.

It turned out that this individual had never invested in self-storage before. The figures that he projected to me weren't accurate. He left out interest payments as well as an enormous number of fundamental costs, which I wasn't able to recognize, because it wasn't my area of expertise. I ended up completing the self-storages, selling them at massive losses, and losing a lot of money.

My favorite two words in wealth protection are *due diligence*. This means to carefully investigate every single detail of an investment. Double-check, get experts to look at it, speak to accountants and bankers, speak to people in the industry. Go completely around the people that you are doing business with and get outside opinions. If I had done that just a little, I would have saved myself an enormous amount of time and money.

If you want to protect your wealth, be very cautious and careful about what you do with the money once you attain it. As I've already mentioned, the best thing is to invest with experts. I was just talking to a man the other day who works in wealth

---

Brian Tracy's favorite two words in wealth protection:
Due Diligence: To carefully investigate every
single detail of an investment

---

management. He works for families that have a net worth of $25 million or more. They turn over all their investments to him and his company, and he takes care of every single part of their financial lives, from bank accounts to credit cards to mortgages to savings accounts to loans to home equity—and of course investing. Because he and his company are so sophisticated, they generate 10–20 percent per year return on their investments, and their clients get richer and richer. Usually they charge about 1 percent as the total management fee for the amount.

If the amount goes up or the investment goes up, it's 1 percent across the board. They generate very high returns, which the average person can't do. The average person has to realize that the only thing that's easy about money is losing it. If you're going to accumulate money at a certain point in life, probably around the age of fifty, you have to start gearing back down again.

You can take a lot of risks when you're younger, you can really work hard and be aggressive, but at the age of fifty you start to step it down a bit and start to be more cautious and more careful. Remember, don't lose money. If you have the slightest possibility that you're going to lose money, just stop and say, "Wait a minute, can I afford to lose this?" If the answer is no, don't do it.

Financial success does open you up to litigation.

One problem that we have today is too many lawyers and too little work for them, so some lawyers go out and try to create work by suing people. Because they are so powerful in the various legislatures, they've gotten laws passed that enable them to sue with no basis at all.

A wealthy friend of mine said, "If you have money, you're going to be sued four times." You just have to take in a deep breath and recognize that if you have something to go after, the lawyers will go after it on straight commission.

If somebody sues you, you have to defend yourself. It may cost $75,000 or $100,000, but if you are sued, you must defend, or the plaintiff will get a summary judgment against you, and you will be found to be 100 percent guilty. Nonetheless, if you want to fight, you have to go through depositions, you have to hire lawyers, you have to subpoena and grill witnesses, you'll have to do many things that are part of the process. If you don't, you don't have a sufficient defense.

Often people have sued me simply because they could. The basis was completely fraudulent, but lawyers are hungry. One lawyer had a standard form. He put in the name of the plaintiff, your name at the top of the page, and his at name at the bottom, and he filed the suit for $250. Now you had to hire a lawyer and defend yourself.

I learned this from a very successful man years ago: Put your money in a place where it can't be touched. Put all of your assets into a family-limited trust. Set it up in such a way that it belongs to your family, although you have total management over the amount. If you put it into a family-limited trust and someone tries to sue you, the lawyers will see how much money you have. If they find it's in a family-limited trust, they'll walk away, because they know they can't get at it.

Let's say they get a judgment for $1 million against you. If it's a family-limited trust that you manage, you can say, "OK, you've got a judgment. I can determine how this money will be paid. We have decided by majority vote in the family-limited

Put all of your assets into a family-limited trust.

trust that we will pay it out at the rate of $10 per year until it's all paid back." They know you can do that, so they won't even sue you. They just walk away. It's a very good tactic, because we live in a litigious society, and many lawyers are desperate for any kind of income. They will sue you on any basis if they think they can shake you down.

It's very important to protect yourself by putting your assets into family-limited trusts. Your lawyers and accountants can show you exactly what to do.

Another key way of protecting your wealth is insurance.

I believe that during your working lifetime, you should have life insurance. You should have straight term insurance, where you buy the maximum amount of benefit for the lowest amount of premium. You should not have whole life or any kind of accumulative insurance, because these are what they call *forced savings*. Most of the money for the first three to five years on a whole life policy goes in straight commission to the agent.

Today most people use the expression "buy term and invest the difference." You can get a much better return if you just buy straight term and put whatever other money you were going to pay into an index fund. Your return will be far greater.

A good friend of mine, a great insurance agent, said that the purpose of life insurance is to guarantee your dreams. If your dreams are to provide for your spouse and kids, even if something happens to you, you buy enough insurance to cover that. You calculate how much would it take to provide for your spouse for the rest of her life.

Instead of investing more money in whole life insurance, buy term insurance, and invest the difference.

Most men think like this, but my friend said that during your lifetime, your job is to reach the point where you don't need life insurance, because you have already accumulated enough so that your spouse has that protection.

As you get older, the cost of insurance becomes outrageous. If you buy $1 million worth of life insurance in your seventies, you may have to pay $500,000 a year for it, so it doesn't make any sense. Your job is to accumulate enough money and put it aside so it cannot be touched by creditors or lawsuits or for any reason at all.

I do not take a stand on disability insurance. Life insurance companies love to sell it, because the agents receive such high commissions. But I think if you properly insure, which you can do through medical insurance and general blanket insurances, you can probably cover yourself for disability. I don't know enough about the subject. I only know that the life insurance agents are very aggressive about selling disability, meaning that it's a very high-profit insurance for them, especially since fewer and fewer people buy whole life. Almost everybody buys term today, and the commissions on term policies are very low.

Some disability policies have low deductibles but are very expensive. Some have higher deductibles, and they're much cheaper. It's like collision insurance for your car. If you have $1,000 deductible, your insurance is going to be much less than if you have a $250 or a $500 deductible.

Long-term care insurance is probably a good idea when you get older. Your children may not be able to take care of you. If you can make sure that you will live in a nice facility for the rest of your life, it's a very smart thing to do. The earlier you do it, of course, the better the rates you can get, because long-term care insurance is based on how long they think you will live once you go into a long-term care facility. After all, their goal is to make a profit. Therefore investigate it very carefully. Look at it, get the opinions of people you respect. Financial advisors and even a good insurance agent will tell you what is good for you and what is not.

For decades, I've had a good insurance agent who looks at every single insurance need and proposal and passes judgment on it from our point of view—the best choice based on our unique situation. It's just like deciding what vitamins you should take or which exercise regimen you need. It very much depends upon you and your situation: whether you're male or female, how much you're earning today, and how much you have put aside. An expert can help you to work your way through all these factors.

Another important tool for protecting you and your family is a will. My wife and I have a will. We've had one for some time, but then the executors changed, the children grew up, moved away, got married, and had children; life changed. We wanted to be sure that our financial situation would be simplified. We went on to the LegalZoom website and downloaded a very simple will just to cover ourselves. We filled in the blanks and gave copies of it to our accountant and to our oldest children, so it's simple, clean, clear, uncomplicated.

Now we want to do a more detailed will. We'll go to an estate lawyer to walk us through twists and turns, because estate law is changing all the time. The government can come in and take

**To protect you and your family, be sure to do a will—
the sooner the better. It makes sure everything
you have accumulated in handed out as you want,
with no argument or disaffection.**

more than 50 percent of your accumulated net worth before there's any disposition, unless you provide against it. You need a lawyer who's current, almost up to the month, with the latest provisions in protecting yourself against hidden taxes.

The last thing you want is for an estate to destroy your family. They say there is nothing that so destroys a family as much as the disposition of an estate. I have seen this up close and personal, where the kids get along fine until a parent dies and leaves some money, which has to be divided up. The children—grown now, in their thirties, forties, fifties—turn on each other like dogs fighting over pieces of meat.

What a parent can do is to be very thoughtful. Before she died, my mother took every single item that she owned—every piece of furniture, jewelry, china, and artwork—and calculated its value. Then she allocated it amongst the four children. She picked my third brother, who is a lawyer, as executor.

When my mother died, we sat down and did the adjudication of the will. Everything was passed out, either on paper or physically. Then each grown child could exchange or barter items with the others. There was never any argument or disaffection, because my mother had thought things through carefully. She didn't want people fighting over single items.

That's a very important thing to do as a parent. You should start by the time you're sixty or sixty-five. Planes run into mountains, and cars crash. You should protect your family by making sure that everything you've ever accumulated is carefully handed out.

Another hot subject today is end-of-life discussions. Once you reach sixty-five or seventy, you should open up the discussion—which your children won't like; they don't want to think about you dying. But you should open it up and say, "We will not be here forever, so if something were to happen to me, to him or her, or to both of us, these are some things that you might think about."

Open up the subject so it's not a hush-hush topic that people creep or tiptoe around: it's just a normal and natural part of life. Then, even without the end-of-life discussion, your kids can say, as mine do, "When you die, can I have this? Can I have that?"

One daughter wants something that's really important to her. The son wants something else, and another child wants something else still. These are good things to get onto the table. It gives you a tremendous sense of peace and comfort to know that you've provided for all of this.

Working people rely heavily on their streams of income. They may wonder how they can protect it against a job loss. I have no idea how an employee who is earning a living and who loses a job can protect against that loss, except by starting early, accumulating savings, and having reserves of two to six months or more equal to their monthly income. There's no other way that a person can do it than by accepting personal responsibility. It's a matter of saying, "If something untoward were to happen, if I were to be incapacitated for a period of time, I have to have this amount of money put aside to provide for me, and the longer the better."

One form of disability insurance is called *loss of income insurance*. You can say, "I need X thousand dollars per month." You can buy a policy for that amount in case you lose your job. However, the policy does not kick in for six to twelve months. The insurer has no desire to give you that money. You have to be either disabled, unable to work, or unemployed for a long period of time before they'll start giving you those payments. Statistically, they know that you'll probably be back at work well before that time.

For business owners, there are different forms of incorporation to consider: sole proprietorship, LLCs, S corporations, C corporations. I'm often asked which one the owner of a new business should use.

The sole proprietorship is the simplest. You could just name the company after yourself, and you're in business. A sole proprietorship means that everything that you put into the company as an investment and everything you take out is taxable. It's like a complete flow-through corporation.

An S corporation is similar, but here you could take on debt such as bank loans. You can hire staff, lease offices—you can run it just like a huge company, and still all the S corporation's net income flows to the owner each year. I have an S corporation. If you have 50 percent of the company and two other people have 25 percent, and the company earns $100,000, that money automatically flows through to your taxable income, and you must pay taxes on it.

A C corporation is different. A C corporation can accumulate money, but you have to pay corporate taxes. Let's say your company earns $100,000. Corporate taxes in the United States are currently 21 percent. You'll have to pay that amount, leaving you with $79,000 in the company. If you pay that out as dividends to your shareholders, they must pay taxes on it at their own rates. It can be an enormous amount of money. However, you could leave the money in the company, which is what big companies like Apple do. They pay their taxes, and they've got $200 million sitting in the bank account, and they can do anything they want with that.

A C corporation is good if you're going to sell shares. You're going to have a large number of shareholders and investors investing with you and to get a piece of the company. You also hope that the shares will increase in value. A C corporation is good for a larger company.

The challenge with the C corporation is that if you invest money in it and you lose the money, you cannot deduct it against your taxes. But if you invest money in a sole proprietorship, an LLC (limited liability company), or an S corporation, that money can be deducted as a loss. The government allows you to deduct money that you spent in anticipation of earning a profit, except that money put into a C corporation is an investment. If that corporation goes under, you lose all the money that you invested in it without being able to deduct it.

An LLC is similar to a sole proprietorship or an S corporation. It's where two or three or more people get together. They put in their money and, say, buy a piece of property, but all income can be taken out as investment, and all income flows through and is taxable for them.

In the end, I don't think there's really very much difference between these setups. It's really subtle. An LLC has its own ways of accumulating capital, while a sole proprietorship is usu-

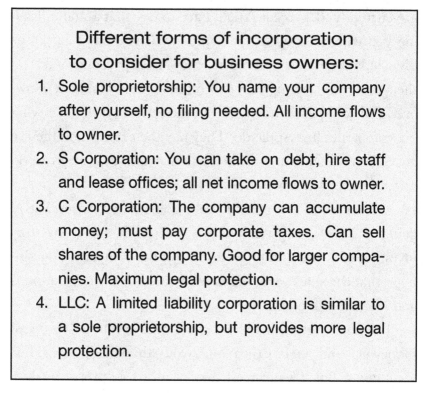

> ### Different forms of incorporation to consider for business owners:
>
> 1. Sole proprietorship: You name your company after yourself, no filing needed. All income flows to owner.
> 2. S Corporation: You can take on debt, hire staff and lease offices; all net income flows to owner.
> 3. C Corporation: The company can accumulate money; must pay corporate taxes. Can sell shares of the company. Good for larger companies. Maximum legal protection.
> 4. LLC: A limited liability corporation is similar to a sole proprietorship, but provides more legal protection.

ally an individual operating on their own, but I do not think that there's any real tax advantage. It's very hard to avoid taxes in our system today. There are 84,000 pages of fine print to capture tax money from you at every single twist and turn.

Again, the only thing that's really different is that in a C corporation, you can invest the money, but you can't get it out. You can lose it all. If you invest money in the other three, that is a cost of doing business and can be deducted as a loss against your current income.

NINE

Money and Happiness

Our overview would not be complete without discussing the controversial topic of money and happiness. After all, what good is earning a great income and creating great wealth if it doesn't leave you happy and fulfilled as a human being?

One great discovery in this arena has to do with how people compare themselves with others. Nobody is either rich or poor except in comparison with other people within their community.

Leon Festinger of Harvard calls it *social comparison theory*. We look at people around us and compare ourselves with them. Researchers recently finished an experiment in which they selectively gave people in a small, poor village community a big chunk of money. Now they were wealthier than their neighbors, and it immediately made the neighbors envious and resentful. People who had been at their same level all the time suddenly had more money; they could buy better things and have a better standard of living. It made the others angry. But over time, the anger subsided, and feelings went back to neutral.

Researchers have also found that when people earn more money, they compare themselves upward. I remember my original goal way back in the sixties, when I started working, was to achieve $100,000. If I had $100,000 (of course, the money was worth much more at that time), I thought that I would really have succeeded. Then I began to meet other people who were worth substantially more. I got into investment sales. People invested $100,000, $250,000 with me, and the investment funds were worth millions.

Then I started to become aware of people who were living in million-dollar houses and had million-dollar incomes. Over time, unconsciously, I began to raise my standards and aspirations for myself. I looked at people earning more than me.

You look for people that are one or two steps ahead of you. You compare yourself with them, and you become discontent. Even so, I wasn't looking at people like Warren Buffett, who were earning billions.

We compare ourselves upward. When people reach their first million dollars, they're happy, but then they start thinking about $2 million. They start looking upward, at people who have $2 million. When you get to $2 million, you look at people who have $5 million. When you get to $5 million, you look

---

Researchers have found that when people earn more money, they compare themselves upward—to those who earn more than them, not to those that earn less.

---

at people who have $10 million. When you get to $10 million, you're looking at people who have $20 million.

People are always striving upward, and this is a healthy thing. I call it *divine discontent*. You strive. Psychologists have found that your level of happiness or satisfaction is directly proportionate to where you are relative to where you thought you should be at this stage of your life.

One of the highest rates of suicide takes place between the ages of forty-eight and fifty-two, mostly in men. It's because they realize that they're never going to make their great financial goals. They're not going to be millionaires. They're not going to be company owners. They're not going to be presidents of companies. For whatever reason, they realize that those aspirations have been dashed, and one day they go home and shoot themselves because of their incredible disappointment. They'd been fooling themselves for years into believing that a miracle was going to happen; suddenly they were going to make a quantum leap.

This is the philosophy of the lottery ticket: one lottery ticket is going to save me from a lifetime of not working, not upgrading my skills, not coming in early, not doing a good job. Somehow I'm going to be saved.

It's the same thing in Las Vegas. It's amazing, the number of poor people who go to Las Vegas, gambling away their grocery money, hoping that somehow the cards are going to come up, the roulette wheel is going to turn, the slot machines are going to kick out the money, and that's going to compensate for years and years of sloth.

Money in itself doesn't make you happy. It's the feeling that you are accomplished at what you do, that you've been able to make this amount of money, that you've been able to provide this well for your family. It's a feeling that you are fulfilling more and more of your potential, and it's measurable. You can see the dollar measure.

Wealthy people will say that up to a certain point, money is just a measure of your ability to cover your cost of living. After that point, you try to hold on to as much as possible by protecting your money and paying as little in taxes as possible.

You can be sure that Warren Buffett is not working for the money. He's working for the pleasure he gets from his work. The money is simply a measure of how well he's doing. If you're an investment advisor, that's a very good measure—how well you're doing for your clients—because that indicates how well you're doing for yourself. So money becomes a measure, and we judge ourselves against this measure.

Abraham Lincoln once said that a person is just about as happy as they make up their mind to be. Each person has a particular level of happiness. It's almost like a thermostat that's set at a given level; they keep going back to that level of happiness.

If a person wins a lottery, their happiness may spike for a period of time, but it will go back to where it was before. Most people who invest in lottery tickets aren't very happy with their lives, so they invest in lottery tickets. A few of them win, and for a while, they're ecstatic. The money goes through their fingers in about two years, and then they're just as miserable as they were before. It doesn't change their lives.

Other people will be pretty happy. Then, say, they lose two legs in an accident. They'll go through the trauma of having lost two legs and being in a wheelchair for life. But after about six to twelve months, they're just about as happy as they had

> "People are just about as happy as they make
> up their minds to be." —Abraham Lincoln

been before the accident. People have an automatic happy stat, if you like, and they keep going back to it.

The goal is to work on yourself and raise that level so you're generally happy most of the time. This requires goals, hard work, becoming good at what you do, good relationships, health, and many other things. It's the decisions you make, which have a lot to do with your upbringing and your level of self-esteem. It has to do with a lot of things that are not controllable in the short term but are controllable in the long term. You can do something about your personality. You can improve your self-confidence and self-esteem.

But generally speaking, people are at a given level of happiness. I look at my four children. They've been brought up with no criticism, high self-esteem, praise, encouragement, and continuous validation by their parents, and they're happy. Anytime, anywhere, under any circumstances, no matter how much stress they have, they're generally happy, optimistic, and cheerful, which means that upbringing does make a difference.

Now if people have a certain standard of living that they're accustomed to, and their income drops and they can't afford that standard of living, that can make them really unhappy. The disparity between where they feel they should be and where they are can cause them anger and frustration.

However, here's what happens. Each person has a self-concept level of income. If they go above their self-concept level of income by more than 10 percent, they engage in throwaway behaviors. They gamble the money, spend it, go on vacations, get rid of it somehow. If they earn 10 percent less than their self-concept level of income, they engage in scrambling behaviors. They start to work harder and longer, upgrading their skills to get back into their comfort zone.

Moreover, people choose their occupations by the way they like to receive money. There are two major ways of receiving income. One is steady, dependable, consistent—weekly, biweekly, and so on. If you like safety, security, stability, and a solid income, without surprises or drama, you seek a job that pays you that way. This is the approach of most people who work today. They much prefer to have a steady, secure income rather than income that fluctuates.

The other way of receiving money is in lumps, which is what entrepreneurs do. Entrepreneurs work six or seven months putting together a deal, starting a business, or turning it around. They'll have big spikes in income, and they're quite happy with that.

In Tom Stanley's book *The Affluent Society*, he said that the time to approach wealthy people is when they have income spikes. If you're selling financial services, property, or real estate, there's no point in talking to them in the slow season, when their business is down. If you ask when they have income spikes and they say, "I make all my money in the last three months of the year," then January is when you talk to those people. This is when they're at their financial peak and they're most open to investing or purchasing.

Another factor is your aspirations. If you're raised in a family with a lot of money, you will aspire to duplicate that level of income as an adult. You're programmed to strive, to upgrade your skills, to work harder, to never be satisfied with a lower standard of living than you were brought up with. This is why many people who come from entrepreneurial households become entrepreneurs themselves. That's their worldview, their self-concept.

Abraham Maslow, the great psychologist, said that we have two types of needs. There are *deficiency needs*, where we're trying to compensate for deficiencies—in safety, security, and belonging. He said we also have *being needs*. We are trying to fulfill our potential. These needs have to do with self-esteem and self-actualization. Maslow said that 98 percent of people have deficiency needs. They are striving to compensate for feelings of inferiority, inadequacy, and frustration. They think financial well-being will compensate for the aching, angry, insecure feeling inside, and they're always astonished when it doesn't.

Very simply, there is no joy in things. All joy comes from relationships, from your interaction with other people. A man could have an incredible year and drive home with a $350,000 Silver Cloud Rolls-Royce. He parks in the driveway and walks in the house. His wife is angry because he was supposed to have phoned a couple of hours ago, and he didn't, so she didn't know whether to make dinner. Now he's arguing with her, and he forgets the car ever existed.

Abraham Maslow's Two Types of Human Needs:
1. Deficiency Needs—compensating for deficiencies in safety, security and belonging. 2. Being Needs—to fulfill our potential; self-esteem and self-actualization.

Another important thing about successful people is optimism. The founders of the most successful, fastest-growing companies all have the quality of optimism. Successful people have off-the-clock levels of optimism about themselves and their company.

Go back and ask, "Why did they start their company?" Because they loved the product. Now they're spending all day long producing, selling, marketing, delivering, and seeing the results from their product. It makes them happy. These people are working longer, harder hours, but they love to work at this. As a matter of fact, it is a deprivation to take them away from their work. It's a punishment.

My partner, Eric, and I joke about how we love to work. We have to use self-discipline *not* to work. Otherwise we'll just keep on working day and night and weekends because we enjoy it so much. If you want to be successful, you have to deliberately decide to take time off. You have to schedule it, and you have to be adamant about not doing anything during that time. Spend time with your family. Spend time on health, walking, or watching television, but take complete breaks. You have to work at it for a while. Then you're OK; you get used to it.

There's another important thing that I teach with regard to productivity. Completing a task gives you a feeling of energy, enthusiasm, and self-esteem. We're designed in such a way that being productive and getting results makes us happy. If we're earning money, we're selling products, we are moving ahead, our business is growing, our customers are happy, we're getting more customers, and making more sales, it makes us happy all the time. It's mainlining happiness.

If you manage your time well, plan your days, work on your most important tasks, and complete those tasks, you get a release of endorphins in your brain, which makes you happy. It gives you energy, makes you more personable, increases your creativity, and strengthens your immune system. Many people who are doing something they really love are mainlining this happiness all the time.

Some may say, "These people are successful, but they're not happy." Well, we've done the research, and the fact is that successful people are very happy. These people have different problems. Which first-class restaurant do we go to? Do we order the filet mignon or the Australian lobster tail? When we go to Paris, do we stay at the George V or at another first-class hotel that costs an outrageous fortune? Do we fly first-class or business? They can say, "I can get this, or I can get that, because I have complete freedom to choose. I have enough money, so I don't have to deprive myself."

Here's another thing that's especially true about self-made millionaires. When a man starts to make a lot of money, his expenditures on himself—clothing, shoes, things like that—stay at more or less the same level. They go up a little bit and flatten out, but his expenditures on his wife and children go up dramatically. Why? Because men get tremendous joy from providing well for their families. They reach a certain level. One pair of shoes is enough; a couple of suits is enough. Men can wear the same things and dress them up by changing a tie or shirt. Women like to have fifty pairs of shoes and a closet full of dresses.

There's a direct relationship between success and happiness, but it has to do with freedom, doing what you love, doing it well,

---

"There's a direct relationship between success and happiness—but it has to do with freedom, doing what you love, doing it well and being acknowledged . . ."
—Brian Tracy

---

and being acknowledged, and then there is the score: you earn more money. You say, "Boy, we're doing well. We had a great week, a great month, a great year, and we were successful." Success makes people happy.

Say you've worked hard and earned a great deal of money; you've had to go through all the work, all the trials and tribulations, to get to where you are. But your kids were raised in relative luxury. How can you raise your children with the same values and work ethic that you have?

The sooner that children can make an association between effort and reward, especially financial reward, the more likely they are to be entrepreneurial. I gave my children allowances, but I also asked them to do some work for it rather than just giving them free money.

Some people say, "Children should be given allowances with no strings attached." That's not building children. Instead, you say, "When you clean up your bedroom and empty the trash, you'll get your allowance." They make an association between completing tasks and earning money.

We live on the golf course of a country club. We have a great slope to our house. The golfers keep hitting balls up onto the slope. Sometimes, because our house is in a dogleg, golfers would try to loop the balls over it, and they would land in our yard. Our kids would collect the balls, sit by the golf course, and sell them for two for a dollar. Golfers would come by, look at the balls, and pick the two they wanted for a dollar. The kids didn't need the dollars. Nonetheless, at the age of ten they made an association between working and making money.

Each of my kids also had part-time jobs when they were growing up, and they did that spontaneously. We have always taken them to the office, where they see us working. They see that Mom and Dad are always working. They make an association between our standard of living and the fact that Mom and Dad work. We talk to them about the work, the business, and our staff. We include them as if they were staff members or shareholders, so that they would feel they were part of a business enterprise.

These are some things you can do to avoid spoiling your children and having them grow up with no connection between hard work and reward.

Today there is a huge amount of talk about the connection between money and happiness. People say, "You should do what you're passionate about. Do what makes a difference in the world."

Now you have a whole generation of people who want to work in nonprofit activities. That's because they're terrified of selling, because selling involves failure and, worst of all, rejection. People go into Internet businesses, because you can't be rejected when you send out a mass Internet mailing.

The sooner that children can make an association between effort and reward, especially financial reward, the more likely they are to be entrepreneurial.

An enormous number of people choose their occupation based on their psychological structure. One quality of healthy people is that they can take failure and rejection and bounce back. They have resilience. Therefore they're willing to try all kinds of things.

With regard to happiness, as I've said, successful people do what they love to do, and they're constantly striving to get better and better at it. Doing what you love to do and getting better at it is one of the greatest sources of happiness. Being able to provide for yourself and your family, being financially independent, are very important.

One fact to note: sometimes you outgrow other people in your family. My wife came from a poor family with ten children. They never had any money, and she now lives in a big house and has a wonderful life. Some of her brothers and sisters have been snide, sneering, and demeaning of her because she has been so successful.

You may also find that this happens with friends. As you develop and become more successful, you may find you have less and less in common with the people you went to school with or hung out with when you started your career. They're still watching TV and having a good time, but this is no longer your worldview. Sometimes you even have less and less in common with your spouse.

Your worldview is that you like to be productive. You like to be producing something. You like to be getting results, because it makes you happy and it opens up all kinds of opportunities and possibilities for you.

Finally, the most important thing that I teach people—and I've practiced it all my life—is to imagine you could wave a magic wand and make your life perfect in every way. What would it look like? How would it be different from today? What would be the first step that you could take to achieve that future dream?

The first area has to do with your income, business, and career. If you were earning the kind of money you wanted to earn, doing the kind of work you love to do, with the kind of people that you enjoy, selling a product that you believe in to customers that you like—if your life were perfect in these ways, what would it look like? How would it be different from today? What's the first step that you could take to begin moving from where you are today to that perfect future?

The second area has to do with your family and relationships. If your relationships, family, lifestyle, home, vacations, everything, were beautiful, how would they be different from today? What's the first step you could take toward that goal?

Third, look at your health: if your health was perfect, if you were absolutely supremely healthy, fit, lean, trim, the best you could possibly be, how would that be different from today, and what would be the first step you could take to move toward that goal?

Finally, your financial situation. Can you determine exactly how much money you would need coming in each month from your investments to be able to retire and never have to work or worry about money again? How much would that be? What's that number? Set it down as a goal, and project forward to when you would want to have it. Then go back to the present and ask, what's the first thing you would have to do to start accumulating to reach that magic number?

Now here's an interesting discovery. People who do this do not think about not working again, because they want to con-

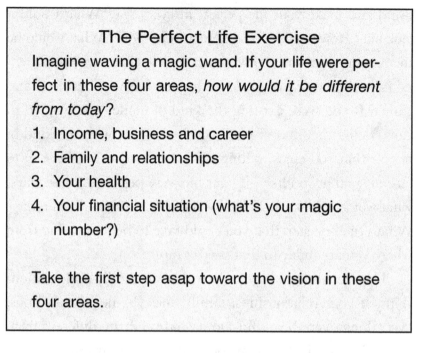

The Perfect Life Exercise

Imagine waving a magic wand. If your life were perfect in these four areas, *how would it be different from today?*

1. Income, business and career
2. Family and relationships
3. Your health
4. Your financial situation (what's your magic number?)

Take the first step asap toward the vision in these four areas.

tinue working all their lives. They just want to have the choice. They want to be able to choose not to work.

So pick your number. Do you know that 80–90 percent of Americans don't know what that number is? Sit down and analyze your total expenses per month, both fixed and variable. Look at your bills. Look at your payments. How much would it cost you to live if you had no income coming in? That's the magic number. How much would it cost per month, per year?

Then you multiply that annual number by 20, because you can assume that you can draw down 5 percent a year without eating into your capital. If it costs you $5,000 a month to live, that's $60,000 a year. Multiplied by 20, that's $1.2 million. At that rate, you could draw down $5,000 a month for 20 years without running out of money. If you need more, calculate it out. Work it out. Write it down, and start striving toward that number today.

The very act of being clear about what your perfect life would look like in those four areas, and then taking the first steps and starting to move toward them, will make you happy.

TEN

Rules for a Vibrant Economy

believe it is our duty as responsible citizens to know what it takes to make our economy thrive for decades to come. I was confused about economics when I was growing up, and if you're confused, you're very easily manipulated by political rhetoric and demagoguery. In fact, most of modern politics depends upon the economic ignorance of the populace.

There's a story about a king who became very wealthy. He decided to collect all the wisdom of the world. That would be his legacy. He sent out his wise men all over the world with unlimited budgets to bring back the collective wisdom of mankind. They came back with 100,000 books. By this time he was fifty or fifty-five years old. "That's too many books," he said. "You've got consolidate it down."

The wise men got together, consolidated, and finally came up with 1,000 books, but by this time he was sixty years old. He said, "I can never read 1,000 books, so you've got to consolidate them down."

The wise men worked for another ten years and condensed the knowledge down to 100 books. Now the king was in his seventies, and he was creaking. He said, "It's still too much. Can't you summarize it even more?"

Again the wise men went away, and five years later, they came back to meet with the king. The leader of the wise men had one little piece of paper in his hand. He said, "We've been able to summarize all the wisdom of all the ages into one piece of paper, and here it is." The king opened it up, and it said, "There ain't no free lunch."

This is the great principle of economics: there ain't no free lunch. In the Western world today, we have Santa Claus economics, something-for-nothing economics. Politicians use the public purse to buy themselves into office, then they raise taxes to use the public purse to keep themselves in office. Politics today is log rolling. You vote for my expenditure and my taxation, then I'll vote for yours: one hand scratches the other person's back, and vice versa. Politicians get into office by promising to give free money to other people—Santa Claus. Just watch: every election somebody is running as Santa Claus.

Every so often an adult stands up and says, "Where's the money going to come from?" Others boo this person down. "The government will pay." But governments have no money except what they extract from the private sector.

Imagine a swimming pool. A government employee takes a bucket, dips it in one end of the pool, runs around to the other

The Great Principle of Economics:
There ain't no free lunch!

end, and pours it back in. That is exactly what governments do. They take money out of one end, from one person or group, and then pour it back in, but there's no net gain in the economy.

But here's the worst thing: because government servants are sloppy, they spill 80 percent of the water, so that the amount of water that actually gets poured back in is substantially less than they picked up in the first place. As government expenditures go up, national wealth goes down. Unemployment goes up and wages flatten out as government expenditures go up, because government is basically a dead weight on the society. Government produces nothing of value that people want, because if people wanted it, the private sector would produce it.

The mayor of Indianapolis had a way of transforming the city's debt-ridden economy. He called it the Yellow Pages test. He said, "If there is any function that the government performs and three or more companies perform it in the private sector, it's going to be farmed out." The public sector unions were hysterical, because they are paid extremely well. They're bankrupting virtually every city, state, and county government in the country with trillions of dollars of unfunded liabilities.

But the mayor stuck to his plan. If this city needed trash hauling, fire hydrant maintenance, or gardening for municipal parks, and if there was a company that did these jobs, he put them out to bid. Surprisingly, the government unions came back. They had to bid in competition with the private sector, and their prices went down. The government unions began to lay off their own lazy people. They began to do the jobs, and do them well, and at competitive prices.

Many years ago economist Henry Hazlitt wrote a treatise called *Economics in One Lesson,* based on Frederic Bastiat's essay *What Is Seen and What Is Not Seen.* He said what you see is the result of government expenditure. Governments hire employees. What you don't see is that for every person that the government hires, two people must lose jobs in the private sector. You see that the government has created all of these new jobs, but you don't see the jobs that disappeared because businesspeople either laid people off or didn't start businesses in the first place because their taxes were too high. These are all standard economic principles.

One politician was confronted with this question: "Do you know anything about basic economics? You can't take out what you don't put in. You can't consume what you don't produce. There ain't no free lunch."

The politician replied, "I know nothing about economics, and I don't want to, because if I did, it would change the way I voted." This is the disease that we have throughout the Western world.

Japan has tipped into recession. Decades ago, it was the third most prosperous country in the world. Then the government brought in taxation, regulation, and expenditure programs and strangled the economy. This is happening now in France.

In the US today, more companies are dying than are being formed for the first time in American history. It used to be that more and more new companies were formed, and a certain number would die through attrition each year. Today it's reversed.

Our entrepreneurial and corporate sectors are dying out. Companies today are not expanding; they're leaving their money overseas, or they're leaving it in the bank. Apple has $200 billion. They sit on it because it's not safe to invest it, because the government will take it away with regulations, taxation, and new laws. Basically Apple has a whole team of lawyers and accountants protecting their money from the government. People are not willing to take risks.

That's our problem in economics today. The Santa Claus politicians are offering something for nothing—money that people have not earned and do not deserve—and buying votes with it. Every time they buy a vote, the next election they have to up the ante and offer even more. Otherwise the public, which is very fickle, will switch its vote to someone else who does.

Right now our national debt is at unprecedented and unsustainable levels. This debt bomb is taking the disease of something for nothing to a national level. This debt is money that is borrowed from the public in the form of government bonds, but ultimately it has to be paid back. The people who know nothing about economics say, "We owe it to ourselves, so we don't really owe it." Yes, we do.

Today we have extremely low interest rates. If our interest rates were running at 4 or 5 percent on a government debt of over $31 trillion, that would work out to about over $1 trillion a year in interest. The country would go bankrupt. That's why

---

"The debt bomb is taking the disease of 'something for nothing' to a national level." —Brian Tracy

---

they are fighting desperately to keep interest rates as close to zero as possible until they get out of office.

For people who work in the private sector and have pensions, the pensions are tied to the stock market. People who work in the government have pensions as well, but they are not tied to anything. They're guaranteed unconditionally for life, and they are altered on the basis of inflation. Even if the economy goes to hell in a handbasket, the politicians will end up with golden parachutes, fabulous pension benefits, and medical benefits that will be adjusted upward, so they'll always be earning more money than when they left office.

A politician who serves two terms in Washington will retire, I believe, with more than $1 million in pension benefits. Plus they'll have a Cadillac medical plan for life. Where's the money going to come from? They don't want to talk about it.

In the eighteenth century, King Louis XV of France is supposed to have said, "Après moi, le déluge," which means, "After me, the deluge." It'll all be over. "Fifty years after I leave office, all these chickens will come home to roost, all the bills will be payable, but I'll be gone."

According to *Business Week*, the amount of unfunded liabilities, the amount that we owe not just in the national debt, but in Social Security, Medicare, pensions, and everything else that is unfunded, is closer to $107 trillion. This is about six times what the country earns in a year, so it can never be paid off. We are the most affluent country in history, and we owe so much debt it's crushing.

Many countries, for example Estonia, have no debt at all. We have more debt than all the other countries in the world put together. The only solution politicians think of is to increase the debt limit: borrow more money that will never be paid back.

Some say that because the US dollar is the reserve currency, we can continue to print money, and other people will hold it. The only thing we have going for us now is that almost every other country is politically more unstable. That's why more and more money comes to the United States, because it's safer here, it's protected by law, so they will continue to punt for a long time. But higher interest rates are coming down the bend. Higher rates on this amount of debt are going to consume the discretionary spending available to the federal government. It's going to wipe out the entire defense budget, along with health, education, and welfare, unless they raise taxes by hundreds of billions and maybe even another trillion dollars.

In 1835, the French statesman Alexis de Tocqueville published a book called *Democracy in America*. He discussed why America was so successful in the early days. It points to areas where we may have fallen short in recent years. He contended that America was made up of individualists, people who accepted individual responsibility for their own work. It was also made up of communitarians in that people cooperated together in activities like barn raisings and crop harvesting.

De Tocqueville said that there is no elite in America, no landed aristocracy. America was set up so that average people could come here, start with nothing, and by dint of hard work and entrepreneurship, create a wonderful life for themselves.

De Tocqueville also saw that the government at that time was extremely small, whereas the governments in Europe were enormous, overwhelming, and oppressive. This led to revolutions and mass murders. There were revolutions in France,

---

Alexis De Tocqueville's vision in *Democracy in America*: America was set up so that average people could come here, start with nothing, and by dint of hard work and entrepreneurship, create a wonderful life for themselves.

Germany, and Italy. There were eventually revolutions in Russia, where the working class rose up because of taxes and oppression.

We never had that in the United States, which was set up to be antiaristocratic. Nobody is better because they come from a wealthy family. Imagine that Bill Gates came up to you and said, "I'm Bill Gates, and I'm one of the richest men in the world. Here, kiss my ring." Imagine if he said that even to an immigrant, a poor person, or a street person. Nobody in America would kiss the ring of someone just because he's one of the richest men in the world.

Today we're losing this sense of individuality and independence. More and more people are becoming dependent upon the government and saying, "Why doesn't the government do this?"

I'll tell you a quick story. Alabama is very famous for having boars. These boars were vicious creatures. They were out in the woods, and nobody went out there because the boars would kill dogs and hunters.

One day a farmer drives into this area and stops at a little town. He said, "I want to catch me some of them boars."

The people said, "No, you don't want to go near those boars. If we go hunting, we have dogs and rifles, because the boars are so dangerous."

The farmer said, "Just tell me where they are, and leave it to me."

"You'll find them down there at the south end of the swamp."

The farmer went out and was gone for a few days. He came back with a big pickup loaded with boars. They were all alive and oinking, jammed into his pickup shoulder to shoulder.

They farmer stopped to get some gas.

The attendant asked, "How did you get them? Nobody could capture even one of those boars. They're the most vicious animals in the Southern United States."

"It was real easy," said the farmer. "I just took some cornmeal, put it on the ground, and went away. The boars came out, sniffed around, and ate the meal. Then I came back and did it again the second day, and they came out again. Then I started to build a little corral, about ten feet away. They came in, ate the meal, and went away.

"I just kept building up the corral. After a few days, the boars were coming there and lining up, getting ready for their free food. Then I closed the back of the corral, and the only place they could go was out the other end, which was the ramp up to the truck. I put a trail of cornmeal right up into the back of the pickup. The boars walked up and got into the back. They jammed in all the way to the end and ate the meal. I closed the back of the pickup truck and drove away.

"It's easy," he said. "You make people dependent for any period of time, and they lose all sense of individuality, independence, and danger. They become meek and mild and easily controlled."

This has been the policy of governments throughout the world: to make people meek and controllable by giving them free things until they become too weak to resist. That's what we're doing, not only here but throughout the world. Most government policies are designed to make people dependent on the government so that they will vote for the government, which promises to keep the gravy train coming.

Everything government does it makes worse, because everything that goes through government is controlled by a political agenda. And the political agenda is always to enrich your friends and punish your enemies. That's why every political contribution is a quid pro quo: I contribute my money, but I expect a big payoff from those politicians if they get into office. You're gambling, putting your money on that horse. If that horse wins, it's going to pay you off. It's going to give you a good ride.

One organization in Washington analyzes the amount of a company's campaign contributions versus the amount of government benefits that company gets over the next four years. Today it's running 72 to 1.

As government grows, the private sector declines. The private sector produces products and services that people want and need and are willing to pay for—actual wealth in the form of cars, clothes, homes, furniture, and cell phones. People consider this to be wealth, because it enhances their standard of living.

Government expenditures on hundreds of thousands and millions of employees who sit around most of the day do not create wealth. Some say that the gross national product grows when we hire more government servants. No, because, again, you have to kill two jobs in the private sector to hire one person to work for the government, and then these people sit around most of the time. *Hard work* and *government employee* never appear in the same sentence.

As government grows, the hopes and possibilities for the people decline. The only way to increase genuine prosperity and opportunity is to decrease the size of government, decrease regulations, decrease taxes. Leave the people to be free; get out of their way.

Most businesspeople in America says, "Just get out of the way. We don't want any government help. We don't want any policies. We don't want anything. Just leave us alone, and let us build and operate our businesses." The world economies that are booming are the ones that have the least regulation and the lowest taxes. The ones that are dying are the ones that have the most regulations and the highest taxes. America used to be the freest nation in the world. It's now number nineteen. It's just below Botswana.

In his book *Trust: The Social Virtues and the Creation of Prosperity*, historian Francis Fukuyama showed that the economies that had the highest levels of trust were also the most prosperous. The economies that had the lowest level of trust were the most impoverished. Economists have done indices on ease of doing business as well. The economies where it's the easiest to start a business are the most prosperous; those where it's the most difficult to do business are the least prosperous. Transparency International also says the countries that have the most corruption are the least prosperous; those with the least corruption are the most prosperous.

"The only way to increase genuine prosperity and opportunity is to decrease the size of government, decrease regulations, decrease taxes." —Brian Tracy

---

For several decades after World War II, the United States led all these indices. Now it's running number nineteen. It's even running number eighteen or nineteen in terms of educational attainment. We spend more per student than any other country in the world, yet we have the worst outcomes.

We need leadership that can stand up and say, "This is not good. We have to reverse it; we've got to start making it easier for people to work, start businesses, and trade nationally and internationally." Until we do that, there's no government policy that can possibly help.

There's been a great deal of discussion recently about the top 1 percent versus the 99 percent. Many people believe that capitalism is at a cancerous stage, where the rich keep getting richer and everyone else will continue to stay the same or get poorer.

As I said before, capitalism is actually savings-ism. If you imagine a primitive farmer who plants a seed and brings in the harvest, what does he do with the crop? He puts seed aside for planting the next year; that seed is taken away from the amount of food that he and his family can consume. In other words, he deprives himself and others. He saves his money. He sacrifices. He practices delayed gratification. Throughout all of human history, these have been the qualities of success.

In the same way, if you work hard, earn money, save some of that money, and invest it carefully in something that generates revenue, you are becoming a capitalist, which means a savings-ist. Where there are no savings, there is no capital accumulation, and there's no future for the nation.

The word *capitalist* came from Karl Marx, who did not understand cause and effect. He just saw wealthy people, but wealthy people save their money and reinvest it. There's an enormous amount of risk and high levels of failure. Sometimes there are long periods of time before there's a return.

If you build a factory, the factory may cost you three to five years to build and another three to five years to make a profit, so you have to be willing to invest for a ten year period before you start to make money. Critics say, "Look at this wealthy son of a gun, making all this money from manufacturing these products, marking the products up three, four, or five times, and ripping off the poor consumer."

What about the ten years that person invested to build the factory in the first place? A small business takes seven years to reach profitability. The day it does, the tax people are in, and they want 50 percent of your profits, because they have no understanding of cause and effect.

The problem with inequality in America is that people don't save their money. They're taught to spend it on fun, big televisions, going to Las Vegas. Every state now has legalized gambling, so if you can't go to Las Vegas, you can gamble right where you are.

Savings means depriving yourself of the joy of consumption today in order to enjoy a higher level of consumption in the future. Savings means putting off into the future the consumption that you could enjoy today. It is only the willingness of people to do that that makes a civilized society possible. Countries where there's no security or safety for savings—corrupt countries, dishonest countries—are countries where people don't save.

The United States is such a safe place to invest because money is carefully protected by law. You cannot steal money without going to jail. In other places, you can steal with both

Where there are no savings, there is no capital accumulation, and there's no future for the nation.

hands and live in a palace on the hill; you can buy off the politicians, judges, and courts, which causes these countries to be in such terrible shape.

You cannot consume what you don't produce. The job of government is to create an environment where the natural, spontaneous entrepreneurial instinct of individuals will lead to the development of new products, services, and businesses. These businesses will hire people, creating jobs and opportunities and paying more taxes, which pay for schools, hospitals, universities, and roads.

That's basic economics. We are living in cloud-cuckoo-land, thinking that it's possible for government to strangle the private sector without any long-term effect. The politicians expect to be out of office and living on fat pensions before the chickens come home to roost.

With regard to income inequality, most people are unequal by choice. They stopped upgrading their knowledge and skills decades ago. They had bad influences or no influences. They did poorly in school, for whatever reason. They came out illiterate. Fifty percent or more of high school students in America graduate illiterate and are unable to fill out an application form to work at McDonald's. Fifty to sixty percent of university students who are admitted have to take remedial courses in English and math during the summer in order to be able to take basic 101-level courses in the fall. These people have no skills. They can't read. They can't operate computers. They don't understand science, mathematics, or engineering. They have no knowledge of business, management, or marketing. They have no way to create value. They have no earning ability, and as a result their incomes are lower.

As Gary Becker of the University of Chicago said, we don't have an income gap; we have a skills gap. The people in the bottom 80 percent have not improved their skills for decades. They came out, worked for one year, and never read a book. The people in the top 20 percent are always upgrading their skills and increasing their value, so the inequality is self-inflicted. Each person decides to be equal or unequal by whether or not they work on themselves and increase their ability to contribute value to their fellow man.

"We don't have an income gap; we have a skills gap."
—Gary Becker, University of Chicago

When a person says, "I've been working at McDonald's for ten years. I'm thirty-five years old. I'm getting $8 an hour, and I've got seven children with no husband at home," whose fault is that? Who made the lifestyle choices that led her to that situation? Individuals are responsible for their own lives. As soon as you take away the idea of responsibility, society falls apart. Actually, the society only stays together because so many people *do* accept high levels of responsibility and don't blame their problems on others.

One common concern today is automation and whether technological advancements will take jobs away from people.

There have been waves of automation since the beginning of the Industrial Revolution around 1770. With every single one, there was a huge outcry: this is going to destroy jobs and leave people in the streets. Yet automation systematizes simple, boring jobs. It frees people up to do higher-order work that is more enjoyable and challenging. Automation creates more jobs.

When the automobile came out, the practice was to manu-facture cars using teams, so an automobile plant may have had twenty or thirty teams, each of which was working on a car. When industry came up with the production line, automation, and scientific management, car factories were able to hire hun-dreds and thousands of people. Hundreds of car factories grew up to employ tens of thousands of people at higher standards of living, with better wages, and better health care.

For the first time in history, a man could afford to work and his whole family could stay at home. Up until that time, the whole family had to work, the kids begging, the mother working in the fields, the father working at a crummy job. But with automation, suddenly one man could provide for his whole family, his kids could go to school, and his wife could stay home.

Every time a job is automated, it frees people up to do higher-level work, and that is one of the blessings. If it weren't for automation, we'd all still be living on the farm. At the turn of the twentieth century, 50 percent of Americans lived on the farm, feeding the other 50 percent. Today less than 1 percent of Americans live on the farm. They feed 330 million people, and they export shiploads of surplus food all over the world to both

At the turn of the twentieth century, 50 percent of Americans lived on the farm, feeding the other 50 percent. Today, 1 percent of Americans live on the farm.

rich and poor countries—because of automation. Automation is a great thing, but it requires you to continually upgrade your skills.

In mathematics, there are certain principles that, once understood, enable the mathematician to solve complex problems that would be impossible for the average person. In mechanics, there are certain proven principles that enable a skilled craftsman to repair an automobile or an airplane using methods, processes, and tools that would be difficult for an untrained person. Similarly, in economics there are certain laws that explain human behavior and which are essential for the entrepreneur to understand.

The fundamental law of economics is the *law of scarcity*. It says economic goods have value because the available supply of them is smaller than the amount that is desired. In other words, there are never enough houses. There are never enough cars. There are never enough diamond rings, beautiful watches, or luxurious clothes. Scarcity gives value to everything. This idea that there should be a surplus, that everybody should be have all they want of some good, guaranteed by government, is nonsense. There will always be scarcity.

In economics, you must continually choose among various options, because you cannot have everything you want. Only little children stomp their feet and have tantrums, crying, "I want this, and I want that." You always have to choose, because your ability to purchase things is always limited. Moreover, because goods are scarce, trade-offs are always necessary. This is the great law of economics that governs societies: you cannot give everything to everyone at all times under all conditions. There just isn't enough.

The second law is the *law of supply and demand*. This says that the price of a good or service is in direct proportion to the available supply relative to the demand at the point of acquisition. The wage, for example, of a fast-food worker, which is basically a commodity, is determined by how many people are willing to work at fast-food places for minimum wage. Because people have no other skills, they are willing to work by the millions at those places.

If somebody says, "I won't work for less than $15 an hour," they will be replaced in about five minutes by a whole list of people who line up to get jobs at that place for $8 or $7.75 an hour, because of supply and demand. There's no objective price. It's always based on how much people want something and how much they are willing to pay.

The law of supply and demand determines all prices, all profits, all wages, all growth, decline, costs, losses, and the success or failure of every business. It's the same with any company that exports. It's always supply and demand. Successful entrepreneurs work continually to increase the demand for what they are selling so they can increase the price they charge. This is what advertising, marketing, and promotion are aimed at: increasing demand.

Another principle is that entrepreneurs continually seek to provide their products and services better, cheaper, faster, or more conveniently so that they can increase the demand for them. That's the basic law. The law of scarcity: everything is scarce. The law of supply and demand: price is determined by how much people want it. As I said before, the number one reason companies go broke is that nobody wants the product at that price.

The *law of substitution* in economics says certain goods and services can be substituted for each other when the ratio of supply and demand for them changes. I'll give you an example. When beef becomes too expensive, people buy chicken. When gasoline prices become too high, people buy smaller cars. When labor prices become too high, companies automate and replace workers with machines. It's always a cost-benefit relationship. If I buy a machine and it saves me a certain amount that I pay in wages, I can earn more in the long run, and that's a good investment.

Customers always have three choices in the marketplace: they can buy the product or service offered, they can buy something from some other company, or they can refrain from buying anything at all. In the marketplace, your customer always has those three choices: buy from you, buy from a competitor, or not buy anything at all. This is the *law of substitution*.

The *law of connectivity* is another great economic law. It says various products and services are connected to one another in either a positive or a negative way and directly or inversely affect the price of each other. When the price of an item goes up, it often causes the price of something connected to it to go up as well. Food price increases lead to restaurant price increases. If you can't get prime rib at the best restaurants, it's because beef prices have gone up. That's because the price of corn, which is used to feed beef cattle, has also gone up. Why can't you get prime rib? It's because all of these prices are connected.

When the price of an item goes up, it causes demand to go down. When restaurant prices go up, the number of people going to that restaurant is likely to go down. Conversely, the number of people going to fast-food restaurants may increase if the prices in expensive restaurants go up.

Everything is interwoven with everything else, so the price of one item affects the cost of others, creating a domino effect. If people stop going to a restaurant, the restaurant buys fewer food products. If a business stops selling more of its product, it cuts back on labor and raw materials—again, connectivity.

There's a story about a guy who has just commissioned a painting from an artist because his business is doing very well. He goes into a restaurant, and sees a poster on the wall. It's from a newspaper that says hard times are coming: the economy is about to drop; we're going to have recession, depression, and unemployment.

The man thinks, "Geez, I hadn't even thought about that. Here I've paid all this money for this painting." He goes to the phone, calls up the artist, and cancels the commission. The artist had just called someone to paint her house, because she thought she had the money for that. Now she cancels that job. Then the housepainter calls the car dealer, because he had just gotten this painting job and was going to get a new car. It goes like this all the way through the economy.

A couple of days later, the first guy goes back into the restaurant and looks a little closer at the poster. He finds that the poster was put up and framed twenty-five years before.

The point is that the wrong piece of information can lead to a connectivity like this, which has a cascading negative effect. That's why whenever unemployment is up, the stock market drops. People sell their shares; they run for cover. Then the experts say, "Unemployment isn't that bad," and the shares all rush up again. The whole stock market is affected by news.

Everything is interwoven with everything else, so the price of one item affects the cost of others, creating a domino effect.

The next law is called the *law of marginality*: all economic decisions, and therefore all prices and costs, are determined by the *last* purchasing decision made. This is an important thing to understand. The amount that the *last* customer will pay for the *last* item available determines the price of the whole supply. Let's say you sell donuts, and the hungriest person, who wants donuts more than anything, will pay a dollar apiece for them because he wants them so badly. But you can't sell your donuts at a dollar apiece, because only a few people would pay that amount. You have to sell your donuts at a much lower price so that more and more people can come into your market. You charge a price that is low enough but on which you can still make a profit. Let's say you get the price down to 50 or 25 cents a donut. Then everybody can have donuts—as long as you're making a profit at the last available sale.

The principle of marginality says it's not that what one highly motivated customer will pay, it's what the last discriminating, careful, cautious customer will pay that sets the price for what you offer. It's always the last customer who can buy that product or buy it somewhere else that sets the price. If I can get it somewhere else for 25 cents and you're charging 26 cents, I'll go to that other place. The *market clearing price* is the price at which all customers will satisfy their needs and all sellers will sell their products and services.

Farmers bring their produce to sell at farmers' markets. Their goal is to have an empty stand at the end of the day, so that the last customer buys the last product from the last stand, and everybody goes home. Everything is sold. That is the market clearing price. You price at the market clearing price for the *first* customer of the day so that by the end of the day, everything has been sold. The principle of marginality is essential to all pricing.

The next law is called the *law of decreasing returns*, which is important both personally and in business. It says the returns, rewards, or profits from some economic activities decrease over time. It says you can often earn high profits from the first products or services you sell. The cost of producing those products or services, however, can increase, and later you could earn fewer profits on the product or service, because your costs have become much higher. There are many activities that you engage in that have a decreasing value. The more of them you do, the less value they have to your customers.

Conversely, there is *the law of increasing returns*. Here the profitability of a product, service, or activity increases as you produce or offer more of it. This, by the way, is the reason for the success of mass manufacturers. In the retail sector, Walmart increases their returns because they buy more and more products— hundreds of thousands, millions—and spread them over 11,000 stores. They get the prices so low that they become the first-choice source for these products for millions of customers every day.

Knowledge is the real source of competitive advantage today. As you produce a knowledge-based product, you become more efficient with every additional unit. It therefore costs you less to produce each unit, increasing the profits you earn on each unit you sell.

I'll give you an example of increasing returns. I do a seminar called "Twenty-First Century Selling." For me to produce that seminar, it took hundreds of hours of research and years of experience on Wall Street. Now that I've given it and polished it using feedback, I now have one of the best one-day seminars on selling in the world. I've given it over 300 times and charge high fees. If someone says, "We need a sales seminar," I can start in five minutes, because I've paid an enormous price to develop that intellectual product. Now that it's produced, it can be reproduced at a very low price. So knowledge-based products have the benefit of increasing returns. The more of them you sell, the more profitable they are.

The next law—and this is important to our discussion of national and international economics—is called *the law of secondary consequences.* It says that every action has both primary and secondary consequences. For everything that you do, something else happens as a result, and for many things that you fail to do, there's a consequence as well.

Economists such as Bastiet and Hazlitt say the primary consequence is always apparently positive. A teenager says, "I'm going to drop out of school, get a job and a car, and have girls." The primary consequence is positive. He's cool, he's got a car, he's got girlfriends. What are the secondary consequences? Lack of education, a low-level job, high risk of unemployment throughout his life, no skills in automation. Eventually he's poor. This is one of the great problems in our world today: an enormous number of people engage in activities that have very serious secondary consequences.

Economist Milton Friedman said that the ability to accurately consider what's likely to happen as a secondary con-

---

"The ability to accurately consider what's likely to happen as a secondary consequence is the key to excellent thinking." —Milton Friedman, Economist

---

sequence is the key to excellent thinking. It's not the *primary* consequence, which is always apparently advantageous. You eat a box of donuts. (I've seen people do this.) The primary result is the deliciousness of the donuts, but the secondary result is that you're going to feel sluggish. You're not going to sleep very well. If you keep doing this over time, you're going to become overweight. You're going to have a big gut. You're going to have to buy clothes that are larger. The secondary consequences of what seemed to be a nice thing to do can be awful.

Next is *the law of unintended consequences*. The ultimate consequences of many actions are far worse than if nothing had been done at all. This explains almost all government policies. It is also a great danger in business. Sometimes an action taken to generate profits generates losses. We can go all in on an investment and end up losing all our money and being far worse off than if we hadn't made the investment at all. Unintended consequences always occur when any action depends for its success on violating the principle of expediency.

The next law, *the law of choice,* says that every human action entails a choice among alternatives, and this choice is always based on the dominant values of the individual at that moment. You always express your true values in your actions. You can tell what a person thinks, believes, and values by looking at what they do, not at what they say or wish.

If you have two types of donuts on the table, you'll always choose the one you want more. If you have two people to marry, you'll choose the one you value the most. It's the same when you have two cars to buy, two jobs to take, two courses to enroll in. By your action, you'll always prove what is most important to you.

This was a shocker to me, because it finally explained why people would say one thing, then do something else, and afterward explain it away: "Everybody does it," or "It doesn't matter." No, what you do is a true expression of who you fundamentally are, so every action you take, or decline to take, is a statement about your values and beliefs. Once I understood that, I understood the world.

Next comes the *law of the excluded alternative*, which says that whatever you choose to do, you're simultaneously excluding all other choices. Every choice implies a rejection of all other choices, at least for the moment. This holds true especially in the marketplace. When you have a choice, you always choose what is most important to you, but in choosing, you reject all other possible choices. When you marry one person, you reject all other people that you could marry (or at least you'd better). Every choice that you make tells yourself and others what you truly believe and value.

The next law—and this is the basis of the entire Austrian school of economics—is *the law of subjective value*. The value of anything is subjective. It is determined by what someone is willing to pay for it, and this explains inequality and why people's incomes are flat and so on. You cannot tell anybody what your job is worth. It's worth what someone else is willing to pay you freely in a free economy when they can choose someone else.

This comes as a shock. All attempts to get above-market rates must use such techniques as government force, legislation, punishment, and fines.

We had a major meltdown in 2008–09. It occurred because the federal government passed laws that made it mandatory for banks to lend to people who had no credit. The politicians hoped that these people would vote for them in the next election. It started under Jimmy Carter. It was expanded under Bill Clinton, and it rolled on like Old Man River under George W. Bush. People were being given money to buy houses. They were buying houses with 3 percent down, and they would get a 3 percent bonus once they moved into them. The banks funded several million homes that people could not afford, and it all came crashing down. It was 100 percent government-endorsed. The government said that these homes have value in and of themselves, when the value was only created by giving people the money to buy them.

All prices set by individuals or businesses are educated guesses about how much people will pay for the item. This brings us to the idea that all sales of merchandise or services at reduced prices are admissions by the vendors that the initial asking price was too high. They guessed wrong.

Only the person being asked to pay for a product or service is capable of determining what it is worth. In a free society, every choice is a free choice. We make it because we feel that we will be better off as a result. Government interference destroys the opportunity for free choice.

The *law of maximization*, the final law that explains economic activity, is that every person seeks to maximize his or her situation in every action to get the very most for the very least.

This is also called the *principle of expediency*. It says that human beings are greedy, lazy, impatient, ambitious, selfish, ignorant, and vain. They constantly strive for survival, security, comfort, leisure, love, respect, and fulfillment. They inevitably seek the fastest and easiest way to get the things they want right now, with little concern for secondary consequences.

All economic activity is built around these principles. All economic results can be explained by reference to these laws, which state that people always strive to get the most for the least, with little or no concern for secondary or unintended consequences

Expecting people *not* to act expediently is simply dreaming. It's like expecting people to change their eye color or expecting them not to breathe and still be healthy.

One example is welfare payments, which has as a primary consequence helping the less fortunate. But too much welfare too long creates the secondary consequence that people become dependent on government. They have no self-respect, no ability to work, no skills. Their income flattens out. They have no hope for themselves, the future, or their children.

If everybody took advantage of these government programs and nobody worked, the society would collapse tomorrow. The only reason it doesn't is that we are hoping that a sufficient number of people will *not* take advantage of these programs, will *not* act expediently, will *not* take the fastest and easiest way to get the things they want with no concern for secondary consequences.

That's my take on economics. There are many more laws, but the bottom line is, as I said at the beginning, there ain't no free lunch. If you apply that concept rigorously to all government policies and activities—and you have to apply them to the private sector as well—then governing would be completely different and much better for all of us and for the future.

There's a saying: remember in times like these that there have always been times like these. No matter how many problems we have in the world today, this is still the best time in all of human history to be alive. Many things are happening politically and economically over which we have no control, so we focus on what we *can* control. Throughout human history, success comes from those who become very good at what they do. They produce a very good product or service that people choose to buy in comparison with similar products and services and buy them again and again.

These people earn a very good living, they save their money, and they invest it in resources that will yield money long after the investment has been made. Eventually, over the course of your lifetime, you reach the point where your invested money is earning more than you are. At that point you can, if you want, begin to back out of your profession or do it differently or do it in a different place. Some people go off and become missionaries and work in foreign countries.

Your job is to take 100 percent responsibility for your financial life and realize that it's totally under your control. Wherever you are today, you can pay off your debts, save money, invest it carefully into income-producing property, and achieve financial independence. If you start right away, it may happen far faster than you expect.

Brian Tracy's
Fundamental Laws of Economics:

- The Law of Scarcity: Economic goods have value because the available supply of them is smaller than the amount that is desired.
- The Law of Supply and Demand: The price of a good or service is in direct proportion to the available supply relative to the demand at the point of acquisition.
- The Law of Substitution: Certain goods and services can be substituted for each other when the ratio of supply and demand for them changes.
- The Law of Connectivity: Products and services are connected to one another in a positive or negative way and directly or inversely affect the price of each other.
- The Law of Marginality: All economic decisions, and therefore all prices and costs, are determined by the last purchasing decision made.
- The Law of Decreasing Returns: The returns, rewards or profits from some economic activities decrease over time.
- The Law of Increasing Returns: The profitability of a product, service, or activity increases as you produce or offer more of it.
- The Law of Secondary Consequences: Every action has both primary and secondary consequences.

- The Law of Unintended Consequences: The ultimate consequences of many actions are far worse (and unexpected) than if nothing had been done at all.
- The Law of Choice: Every human action entails a choice among alternatives, based on the dominant values of the individual at the moment.
- The Law of the Excluded Alternative: Whatever you choose to do, you're simultaneously excluding all other choices.
- The Law of Subjective Value: Something is worth what someone else is willing to pay you freely in a free economy.
- The Law of Maximization: Every person seeks to maximize his or her situation in every action, to get the very most for the very least.

CPSIA information can be obtained
at www.ICGtesting.com
Printed in the USA
JSHW050811080922
30203JS00005B/6